Person County Past

PERSON COUNTY PAST

Tales from the Central Piedmont

PHYLISS BOATWRIGHT

THE History PRESS

Published by The History Press
Charleston, SC 29403
www.historypress.net

Cover Image: Palace Theater on Roxboro's Main Street

First published 2006
Manufactured in the United States
ISBN 1.59629.153.9

Library of Congress Cataloging-in-Publication Data

Boatwright, Phyliss.
Person County past : tales from the central Piedmont / Phyliss Boatwright.
p. cm.
ISBN 1-59629-153-9 (alk. paper)
1. Person County (N.C.)--History--Anecdotes. 2. Person County (N.C.)--Biography--Anecdotes. 3. Person County (N.C.)--History, Local--Anecdotes. I. Title.
F262.P5B63 2006
975.6'573--dc22
2006018716

Notice: The information in this book is true and complete to the best of our knowledge. It is offered without guarantee on the part of the author or The History Press. The author and The History Press disclaim all liability in connection with the use of this book.

Contents

Introduction

I've lived in or near Person County, North Carolina, for the past couple of decades. I have had the pleasure of working here for the past seven years, as a staff writer for the *Courier-Times*, the Roxboro community newspaper that serves Person County.

I have had the honor of getting to know a majority of the folks who populate this place called Person. Along with my colleagues, I have documented the lives of many Personians.

There is a well-used slogan here in Person County. Adopted by the Tourism Development Authority or the Chamber of Commerce or some such entity, "It's Better in Person" has been the subject of snickers by some and derision by a few. It may sound a bit corny, but it is true.

Person County is made up, for the most part, of good, honest, hardworking, down-to-earth people. The countryside could not be more beautiful, with its rolling red clay hills, thick hardwood forests and the deep green of well-kept fescue lawns. Personians take care of their county.

And they value the rich history and heritage of the area. There is so much history here that it is difficult to pick out just a few people and places to write about. So many outstanding, influential and downright famous folks—Enos "Country" Slaughter instantly comes to mind—were either born and raised or at some time lived in Person County.

What I've tried to do in this small volume is focus on what I think are a few of the most interesting landmarks and a few of the most interesting folks. This is by no means meant to be an all-inclusive history of Person County. That would take volumes. I hope, however, that those who read it enjoy revisiting a few of the people, places and events that truly do make it better in Person.

Written by Phyliss Boatwright.

A Brief History of Person County

Located in the northern Piedmont area of North Carolina, Person County is bounded by Durham and Orange Counties to the south, Granville County to the east and Caswell County to the west. Virginia's Halifax County is to the north.

Person County as it is known today was first a part of Edgecombe County in 1746, part of Granville County from 1746–1752, included in Orange County until 1778 and part of Caswell County until 1791 or 1792. By dividing Caswell County into two squares, each side measuring approximately twenty miles in length, two counties of four hundred square miles were formed.

The county was named for General Thomas Person, a Revolutionary War Patriot who made significant contributions to Person County and surrounding areas. He was a trustee of the University of North Carolina, donated large sums of money to the institution and was commemorated by the construction of Person Hall.

The Person County Court House graces the center of uptown Roxboro. Statues on its lawn commemorate Personians who served their country in various wars.

Lieutenant Colonel Stephen Moore was another Revolutionary War hero of note, commanding troops in Person County. The story is told of his riding to the top of a hill, admiring the beauty of the view and vowing to return to his "Lost Eden" after the war. In 1793 he purchased property in the southern part of the county and named it Mount Tirzah (Mount Beautiful) or "General Moore's Mountain." His old home is still located at its original site and owned by a descendant. The front porch overlooks the same inspiring view. Moore was buried on a nearby hill.

Person County was a well-established plantation center before the Civil War. Crops included tobacco, cotton, corn, wheat, oats, fruits, vegetables, cattle, hogs and sheep; many of the same crops grown here today. After the war, the area's large plantations were divided into many small farms.

During the Civil War, Person County supplied eight hundred to one thousand soldiers to the Confederate cause. A granite monument on the Person County Courthouse lawn honors E. Fletcher Satterfield, who advanced the Confederate flag at Gettysburg.

J.A. Long, W.W. Kitchin, A.R. Foushee, J.S. Bradsher, J.C. Pass, W.F. Reade and R.E. Long were key leaders who helped make a transition to a more diversified economic base after the Civil War. The Norfolk and Western Railroad Company was a major influence around 1890, facilitating the addition of tobacco processing plants and warehouses. Although the processing plants disappeared many years ago, a few of the warehouses still stand.

J.A. Long established People's Bank in 1891 and the Roxboro Cotton Mills in 1899, later known as Tultex Yarns. Long died in 1915 but was succeeded by his son, J.A. Long Jr., who began attracting new business to Roxboro. Baker Company opened here in 1923, making textiles a major contributor to the local economy.

Baker was merged with Collins and Aikman Corporation (C&A), becoming a major industry in Person County. C&A will close its Roxboro plants in August 2006, displacing 545 workers and ending a long chapter in the county's history.

Lake Hyco and Lake Mayo are and have been major forces in the economic equation here. Person County contains parts of three major river basins: the Neuse, the Roanoke and the Tar, providing essential clean drinking water to the south and east of the state. Rivers coursing over this scenic plateau and forming numerous valleys include the Tar, Little, Flat, Mayo and Hyco. The area's ridges are not narrow and sharp like those in much of the Piedmont, and the gullies and ditches are not as abrupt. The land gathers into strong swells, small enough to represent the flat plateaus of the Piedmont yet intersecting with wide meadows. Person County claims two small mountains—Mount Tirzah and Hager's Mountain.

Roxboro is the only incorporated municipality in the county, although there are nine townships, many with community centers or postal offices. The Town of Roxboro was chartered January 9, 1855. An annexation in 1998 brought the town's population to eight thousand and the county's latest census registers thirty-three thousand.

Written by the Person County Museum of History.

The "Father of Roxboro"

No history of Person County would be complete without mention of John Anderson (J.A.) Long. Many consider him the father of modern Roxboro.

After all, it was J.A. Long who built the textile mills that would play such an extended role in the economy of the county. He also brought the railroad to town, linking Person County to the rest of the world for trade and travel.

J.A. Long was not born into wealth. He was the archetypal self-made man. Born and raised on a farm, he was the eldest child of Ratliff J. and Mary Walters Long. As the oldest, "Dee" Long would be the one to leave home and serve in the Civil War.

About three months before the end of the war, after serving in over twenty campaigns, Long was captured near Petersburg, Virginia, and placed in a Yankee prison. While imprisoned, he hollowed out buttons and covered them with the gold dollars he earned as a soldier, selling them as rings in order to buy bread.

Ten weeks after the treaty was signed at Appomattox, Long was finally released and made his way back to Person County

J.A. Long was largely responsible for early commerce in Roxboro and linking Person County to the rest of the country via railroads.

on July 3, 1865. He returned to find the family farm deeply in debt. His father had died on June 20, and shortly thereafter, his grandfather Reuben passed away as well, pushing the young J.A. to the head of the family.

Taking on the responsibility for the farm, his mother and younger siblings, Long decided that it was best to let his younger brothers run the farm while he went into town for a paying job.

George Washington Norwood owned a tobacco factory and a store in Roxboro, and J.A. Long got a job there, walking to work and back home. He earned fifty cents a day, but somehow he managed to pay off the debt on the farm. And, two years after going to work in the Norwood store, Long was made manager because of his innate abilities in business matters.

Also that year, J.A. Long married Mary Elizabeth (Betty) Winstead. Betty's mother didn't like her daughter's suitor, so she would only allow the two to go to church together. J.A. would collect Betty on Sunday morning and accompany her to what was then Roxboro Station. But one Sunday morning in 1867, the couple didn't stop at the church. Instead, they went on to nearby South Boston, Virginia, and got married.

Betty was the perfect wife for the ambitious, industrious J.A. Long. She was as interested as he in developing Roxboro, building and achieving. The two worked so well together that they eventually were able to own the Norwood store, changing the name to J.A. Long and Company. Betty worked there until she died in 1882.

The Longs had a son, Robert Edgar, who gave his father the impetus and inspiration to establish a school. Thus, Roxboro Male Academy was founded in 1840. A daughter, Margaret Pearl, was born in 1874.

The Longs built a large, chateau-esque home on Main Street in Roxboro, and during the 1870s and 1880s their hard work

Long Memorial United Methodist Church, named in honor of J.A. Long's son Edgar, is one of the stateliest structures in uptown Roxboro.

paid off. J.A. Long accumulated property and wealth, all the while earning the respect of his peers and townsfolk.

He was the benefactor of Long's Chapel, which is today known as Long Memorial United Methodist Church, and built the Roxboro Male Academy, where he would pay the tuition of some students who couldn't afford to attend the school. He eventually owned the largest mercantile store in Roxboro and when his son was old enough to work there, the name became J.A. Long and Son Company. Long also ventured into other areas of business and managed several farms.

But tragedy struck when Betty Long died in 1882. Knowing she was terminally ill, Betty told her husband that she wanted him to marry her best friend, Laura Thompson of Leasburg. A year after Betty's death, Laura and J.A. were married. They had two children who survived past infancy, J.A. Long Jr. and Matt Ransom Long, who was named after a Civil War soldier. These two sons would join the family business when they were old enough. They also became entrepreneurs in their own right as well.

In 1895, J.A. decided to build Laura a home of her own, a short distance down Main Street from the home he and Betty had built. Today, the Roxboro Savings Bank sits on the former site of that second Long home. The first one still stands and was renovated in 2005–2006 after years of neglect.

During the 1870s, J.A. Long began his fight to bring the railroad to Person County. This was finally accomplished in 1890, when the Lynchburg and Durham line came through Roxboro, joining the town and county to markets both to the north and south.

Long was also one of the organizers of People's Bank, which later became First Union and today operates as Wachovia. He was the first president of People's Bank and guided it through critical times when many other banks were forced to close.

In the mid-1890s, Long worked toward accumulating the capital to bring the first cotton mill to Roxboro. The Duke and Watts families in Durham, as well as Roxboro merchants, invested heavily in the venture and a corporation was formed in 1899.

Following a few years of rough going, the Roxboro Mill, which is today being renovated to house a charter middle and high school, became successful. A second mill was built in 1909 in the community now known as Longhurst. That building today houses the automotive parts company called Strutmasters.

It was J.A. Long who enticed the Baker Company, a cotton velvet weaving industry, to come to Roxboro. The velvet was a built-in market for the cotton yarn spun in Long's plants. The

Baker Company would later be bought by Collins & Aikman, the largest manufacturer of cotton velvet in the United States, which became the county's largest employer and remained so until 2006.

During the heyday of his mills, J.A. Long built mill villages that still stand today. His employees lived in the villages and bought the foods they didn't grow and other necessities at the company store. A timecard at the Person County Museum of History today shows that a worker earned thirty cents an hour in 1939, taking home $2.50 for thirty-three hours of work after rent, tax and his debt to the company store were paid.

J.A. Long died after a period of declining health on April 12, 1915, of pneumonia. He was seventy-four. All businesses in Roxboro closed for owners and employees to attend the funeral.

For years, those who remembered Long said he helped countless people in need, from extending credit to making outright gifts and grants for education.

Written by Phyliss Boatwright.

Sources: The *Courier-Times Centennial Edition, 1982, sec. A12;*

The Person County Museum of History; Mrs. Jean Newell.

Enos "Country" Slaughter: True Hometown Hero

Like J.A. Long, Enos "Country" Slaughter's life is a part of Person County history that cannot be overlooked.

The right fielder, perhaps best known for his "mad dash" to home plate to propel the St. Louis Cardinals to victory in the 1946 World Series, was born on April 27, 1916, in the Allensville community. The five sons and one daughter of Zadok and Lonie Gentry Slaughter all played sports and played them well. But it was Enos Bradsher, the third child, who possessed the "fire in the belly" that would make him a baseball legend.

While the family worked hard on the farm, sports were all-important, and work stopped for ball games. Lonie Slaughter was in the stands at each game, calling out instructions to her children.

In his 1999 autobiography, *Country Hardball*, Slaughter wrote, "My first memories of going to ballgames were with the family by horse and buggy…On special occasions, we all piled into whatever vehicle we were using at the time and rode twenty-five miles south to Durham to watch professional baseball. At those

Enos Slaughter, Baseball Hall of Fame member, was always a Person County country boy at heart.

Bulls games in the old Piedmont League, I began to realize that it was my life's ambition to become a professional baseball player."

After growing up on a tobacco farm and playing on community teams and on the Ca-Vel Industrial League team in Roxboro, Enos Slaughter got his chance at the big time in 1934. A sports writer in Durham recommended the farm boy to the Cardinals, who were holding tryouts in Greensboro. Slaughter was chosen to play in the minor leagues in Martinsville, Virginia, that year, and went to Asheville in 1935.

Slaughter told the *Courier-Times* in 1982, "When I got to Asheville, they had a question mark by my name and said, if I couldn't improve my running, they'd release me." The manager told the young ball player to go to the outfield and practice running on his tiptoes.

"I did it," Slaughter said, "and, in three days, I had increased my running speed to first base by four steps." In 1936, he was picked to go to Columbus, Georgia, to play in the minors, where he hit only .220 in the first half of the season.

"Eddie Dwyer told me," Slaughter said, "'Son, if you ever find the strike zone, you'll go to the major leagues.' I came back to hit .325 for the year." It was at Columbus that Slaughter "started running all the time," beginning his career-long habit of hustling onto and off the field of play.

In 1937, the Cardinals needed a left-handed hitter for their parent organization in St. Louis. Slaughter went to spring training in Daytona, Florida. In 1938, he hit the big leagues and in 1939, he led the National League in doubles, with fifty-two.

In the 1946 World Series between the Cardinals and the Boston Red Sox, Slaughter made his famous race to home plate from first base on a single hit by Harry Walker. Slaughter had been instructed to stop at second, but later admitted that, once he got there, he thought he could make it to third. At third, he thought he could make it home. He did, sliding under the ball onto the base.

During the 1947 season, Slaughter would be caught up in controversy that would follow him the rest of his life and, some say, keep him out of the Baseball Hall of Fame until 1985. After scoring the tying run in the ninth inning between the Cardinals and the Dodgers, Slaughter made a run for first base, spiking Jackie

Robinson, the first African American to play in the Major Leagues, in the ankle.

In his autobiography, however, Slaughter wrote that Robinson stepped forward to "scoop up the throw, and when he stepped back on the base for the putout, his foot was right in the middle of the bag. If I were going to slide like you do when you're headed into second base on a close play, nothing would have happened. But this play was at first base, where a runner is allowed to run past, and the object is to get there as fast as you can. I had always played by the rule that the base paths belong to the runner, and I don't believe I have to apologize for not making an exception to this for anyone. On this occasion, my spikes clipped his ankle."

Slaughter goes on to say that he didn't think much about the accident, given that Robinson was not seriously hurt, until after the game, when, "It was the trash that some writers put into their accounts of this so-called 'incident' that made my blood boil. They claimed I had spiked Robinson deliberately. They even attributed the friction between the Cardinals and the Dodgers to Robinson's presence. Hell, the two teams had been fighting like cats and dogs for the entire decade, but now that Jackie had been promoted to Brooklyn, the writers said the two teams fought because the Cardinals were prejudiced."

When he was finally inducted into the Baseball Hall of Fame, one of Slaughter's daughters wrote a speech for him to deliver. When he reached the podium, however, the man well known for his cryptic comments merely said, "It's about time."

His Major League career spanned nineteen seasons, with a three-year interruption during World War II. In 1943, Slaughter enlisted in the Air Force. In 1954, he was traded away from the Cardinals and sent to the New York Yankees.

He was traded "boom, just like that," Slaughter told the newspaper. "Yes, it hurt me, but I went from the top organization in the National League to the top organization in the American

League." The Yankees and manager Casey Stengel were good to him, Slaughter said, adding, "I think I helped them."

After his retirement in 1959, Slaughter worked with the Raleigh Caps in the Carolina League as a player-manager and then as coach at Duke University, while also returning to the family farm. When Piedmont Technical College, now known as Piedmont Community College, was founded in the mid-1970s, Slaughter coached a start-up team there. Over the years between his retirement and his death in 2002, Slaughter made many personal appearances. He worked with the Person County Museum of History, autographing baseballs and attending museum functions. A room at the museum boasts an extensive collection of memorabilia from his baseball career.

He was also known as a colorful character who never shied from speaking his mind. He ruffled feathers from time to time with his straightforward commentary, but was beloved by his fellow Personians.

When he died, the county was abuzz over the baseball dignitaries who came to pay their respects, among them Ted Williams. His four daughters, Patricia, Gaye, Rhonda and Sharon, gathered around Slaughter's casket and sang, "Take Me Out to the Ballgame" before their father was laid to rest in the cemetery behind the picturesque stone building of Allensville United Methodist Church.

Written by Phyliss Boatwright.

Sources: The Courier-Times *Centennial Edition, 1982, sec. H1; Enos Slaughter with Kevin Reid,* Country Hardball *(Greensboro, NC: Tudor Publishers, 1991); Mrs. Jean Newell and the Person County Museum of History.*

Allensville: Where Enos Came From

The shape of Person County is almost a perfect square: twenty miles to a side. When the county was formed from Caswell in 1792, it consisted of the four townships of St. James, St. Luke's, St. Lawrence and Nash. Today it is equally divided into nine townships. Cunningham at the northwestern corner accompanies Woodsdale and Holloway along the northern border adjoining Virginia. The southern portion consists of the three townships of Bushy Fork in the southwest, along with Flat River and Mount Tirzah. The center three townships, starting in the west, are Olive Hill, Roxboro and Allensville.

As with most of Person County, Allensville has always been primarily an agricultural community. The 1870 Person County census lists a total of 220 households in the Allensville Township with an overwhelming majority involved in farming. Additional occupations also listed were blacksmiths, a Baptist preacher, clerk, wheelwrights, dry goods merchant, carpenters, shoemaker, doctor, schoolteachers and still others involved in agriculture, specifically tobacco, including a superintendent of a tobacco factory.

Even Allensville's most famous personality, Baseball Hall of Fame member Enos Slaughter, reflects the importance of the rural agricultural community in his life, not only with his nickname "Country," but also with his autobiography, *Country Hardball: Enos Country Slaughter, A Farm Boy from Roxboro*.

Perhaps not as famous nationally, but also familiar to Personians, is the musical Gillis Family who hail from the Allensville community. Another Allensville musician of note is piano player Henry Slaughter, a member of the Southern Gospel Piano Roll of Honor.

A plaque reveals that Allensville was a first-place winner of the Farm Division in 1967 and of the Small Community award in 1968 presented by the North Central Area Development Association, again reflecting the role agriculture has played in the community. The Person County Community Development Program also presented another plaque honoring Allensville for its outstanding programs featuring education and community-wide improvement projects in 1964.

Allensville being no different than the rest of the country, during the early part of the twentieth century, schools and churches were the heart of the community. According to a notebook history of Allensville schools compiled by Grace Crow, a group of teachers met on December 10, 1915, at the Sol O'Briant School, and, during the meeting, "The superintendent had a vision of a high school at Allensville with roads radiating in every direction and with great wagon loads of happy, laughing and merry children going to the great school." Discussion was held in regard to consolidating Trilby, Parham and Black Gum schools. As it turned out, a four-room structure was completed in January 1918. Later two more rooms were added, and in 1928, a four-room brick building was erected for a high school.

Allensville United Methodist Church, with its beautiful natural stone facade, is one of the oldest churches in Person County.

Sol O'Briant School was one of the original John C. Terrell schools built with funds from the $100,000 endowment the Person County physician left the county school system at his death. Sol O'Briant was renamed in 1941 as Cedar Grove No. 2.

The O'Briant School, located between Allensville and Surl, was named for Solomon O'Briant, who was born in 1852 and taught at the school for more than thirty years.

In 1952, a state school survey recommended the consolidation of high schools in Person County, and Allensville High School merged with Bethel Hill. The last class to graduate from Allensville was the Class of 1952 with eleven graduates: Mildred Day, Alma Boyd, Alma Melton, Esther Poindexter, Gustavia Gentry, Cynthia

Long, Franklin Lowery, Harold Denny, Sterling Knott, Charles Knott and Gene Flynn. The building, though in very bad shape, is still standing.

A resident student tragically was instrumental in the North Carolina Legislature passing a law making it illegal to pass a stopped school bus. On February 27, 1930, Bessie Yarboro, a twelve-year-old fifth-grade student at Allensville, was killed in front of her home after getting off the school bus.

One of the oldest churches in the county is Allensville United Methodist Church, although it has not always been known by that name. Originally, it was called Bethlehem Church.

From 1885 through 1906, Allensville also had a post office.

The Allensville Grange Number 1072 of the North Carolina State Grange was a farm organization with a purpose to serve not only full-time farmers but also the total interest of the rural community. The Allensville Grange was organized in 1947 by twenty members from the community.

As Caltolina, another small community in the eastern part of the county, was named for the resident Calton family, the Allensville District and community were possibly named after the early Allen family, who lived there in the community's formative days.

The 1794 tax list for Person County shows a Drury Allen Sr. owning 940 acres and David Allen with 1,000 acres. David Allen inherited his father's land and married Catherine Lanier. According to information submitted by Mrs. George M. Allen for publication in *Person County Heritage*, David (1746–1828), son of Drury, and Catherine (1772–1832) are buried in a private plot in Allensville Township on the land David inherited from his father.

Written by Vicki Berry.

Originally appeared in the Courier-Times, *March 3, 2004, sec. B1.*

Miss Bessie: A Modern Woman for All Time

Bessie Heath Daniel was a liberated woman long before the first bra was burned in the 1960s.

Born in 1886 in Person County's Flat River Township, Miss Bessie would have several successful careers in her life, ranging from farmer to secretary to college professor to county agent to radio personality.

Bessie Heath Daniel lived ninety years and each was filled to the brim. Born on the family farm to Lewis Heath and Sallie Barnett Daniel, Ann Elizabeth was named for both her grandmothers. Showing her independent spirit early on, she changed her name to Bessie Heath when she started to school.

She was encouraged by her parents to get an education and attended State Normal College in Greensboro, which is now the University of North Carolina at Greensboro. After completing

Bessie Heath Daniel during one of her radio shows, wherein she offered advice on everything from farming to remedies for illnesses.

her studies, Bessie served as secretary to Dr. Charles D. McIver, the first president of the school. She absorbed his philosophy, it is said, of "Educate a man, you educate an individual. Educate a woman and you educate a family."

Although Miss Bessie never had her own family to educate, she applied the philosophy to all of Person County. Whenever there was a void in the social needs of the populace, according to *Person County Heritage*, she sought to have it filled.

Miss Bessie's mother's health failed in 1909 and she and her sister took turns caring for her. Miss Bessie wrote that her sister was a teacher, so Bessie stayed with their mother during the winter months, and, during the summer while her sister took over, Bessie did "whatever jobs Mr. E.J. Forney, my teacher, assigned to me in various parts of the state."

In 1919, she worked in the Motor Transport Corps of the War Department in Washington, D.C., as a statistician.

"I did not like that work," she wrote. "The individual is too small a cog in too big a wheel in Washington."

She would later teach seventh grade and geometry in the Roxboro School, and at what she called "Hillcrest High School" at Flat River Church.

Around 1920, Miss Bessie worked for the crippled children of Person County. The Missionary Society of what was then Edgar Long Methodist Church (now Long Memorial United Methodist) offered to "foot the bill," she wrote, for necessary expenses in sending children to and from the Orthopedic Hospital in Gastonia. Mount Zion Church organizations paid the expenses for two children. "Both of these girls were wonderfully benefited," Miss Bessie wrote. The County Commissioners became interested and as a result established the Person County Health Department.

Sometime between 1920 and 1925, Miss Bessie, along with Mrs. Mamie Merritt and Mrs. Bob Smith, "went before the

County Commissioners to ask for the first Aid for Dependent Children check ever issued in Person County. In this case the husband and father had been killed in an accident. These checks were used very wisely."

Mrs. Jean Newell, docent at the Person County Museum of History, says Miss Bessie was "a Renaissance woman" who brought many firsts to the county.

On September 8, 1933, Miss Bessie said she "went to Raleigh with the county agent to attend a statewide meeting of county agents. The next day I began work in his office . . . and worked there for twenty-three years." Beginning in 1938, aside from being the first woman in North Carolina to hold the position of assistant county agent, Miss Bessie was also instrumental in getting the first county agent appointed in Person County. As soon as the agent was appointed, she became his assistant. She was also responsible for enticing county commissioners to start a welfare department. *Person County Heritage* notes that in the late 1920s the county was without a county farm agent for some time and Miss Bessie did not like that fact. She wrote letters to Raleigh until the state finally sent H.K. Sanders to Person County. She did the same for the Welfare and Health Departments during the early 1920s.

In 1916, she said, "My first car was a Model T Ford. I bought it from H.L. Crowell [on] March 15, 1916. It looked like a buggy, with oilcloth curtains, and isinglass windows. It had no starter. I bought it for $390." That car would serve her well for years to come.

During the Great Depression, the family farm was mortgaged and in danger of being lost to the bank. To save it, Miss Bessie loaded wood onto her Model T, took the wood to town and sold it. She sold butter, eggs and milk as well to pay off the mortgage.

At some point in time, Miss Bessie did have a male suitor, but she was charged with the care of her parents and could not shirk that responsibility. Her father was paralyzed after a stroke in 1923 and remained so until his death in 1934, so she took charge of the farm and remained in charge until her death in 1976. During her last year of life, Miss Bessie reportedly said, "I have sacrificed my entire life for that farm."

When at age seventy she was forced to retire from the county agent's office, she was so annoyed she never forgave her employers.

"Why I can type and take shorthand as well as I ever could, and I can still advise folks on farming," she said.

Not wanting to slow down, she began a radio program on "the first Friday in September 1956," she wrote in 1972, "and have continued that, which has given me much pleasure." Miss Bessie presented programs that reflected "her vitality, keen intelligence, sense of humor and deep love and interest in the people and the county," according to *Person County Heritage*.

Miss Bessie was tall and stately and always wore a hat. The wide-brimmed hat became known as her trademark, but she wore the hat because her eyes were sensitive to the sun.

Miss Bessie died February 29, 1976, and is buried in the family cemetery at her home, where she had spent much of her long, productive life. Today, a historical marker on the Hurdle Mills Road tells of her devotion to the farm and the county.

Written by Phyliss Boatwright.

Sources: The Courier-Times *Centennial Edition, 1982, G16; Mrs. Jean Newell, Person County Museum of History docent;* Person County Heritage *(1981): 215.*

Bushy Fork Township: A Small Place with Lots Going On

Historically, the Bushy Fork Township has always been predominantly a farming community with close ties to tobacco.

"Tobacco ruled the roost," says Bushy Fork Township resident and farmer Craig Hester. "But of course, you could say that for the county."

Just as farming has long been associated with the Bushy Fork Township, the Hester name has similarly been associated with farming and the general area, as evidenced by one of the Township communities, known as Hester's Store. The Hester family ran a mercantile business in the time when stores were often the heart of rural communities.

Long's store, too, was an institution in the Bushy Fork community, says Bushy Fork resident Bill Hovatter. The store remained in operation until the early 1970s. Early ledgers are a window to day-to-day activities during the early part of the century, reflecting the ordinary items purchased, the price paid and the local resident who made the purchases. For example, one pair of gloves cost twenty cents, two spools of thread were ten cents and a gallon of molasses was fifty cents.

Other important community stores in Bushy Fork included Bayne's store in Gordonton, Whitfield's store in Hurdle Mills and Wilburn's store in Hurdle Mills.

The Hester family was also responsible for the community of the same name when Hester's Store post office began operating in 1854 with Robert H. Hester as postmaster. Soon after, in 1855, the community of Bushy Fork started a post office with William A. Bradsher as postmaster, but that office was discontinued in 1910. However, of all the post offices that existed in the Bushy Fork Township, Gordonton can boast the earliest, which began in 1830 with Alexander Gordon as postmaster. In 1907, the Gordonton post office was discontinued to Hurdle Mills. Hurdle Mills was originally known as Daniel's Mill when the post office was established in 1846 with William Daniel as postmaster. In 1859, the name was changed to Hurdle Mills.

The names of these early communities remain familiar names to Personians today with the exception of a post office community called Hern, located near Hester's Store. In 1902, Charles B. Smith was named postmaster and in 1905, Hern was discontinued to Bushy Fork.

But post offices were not the only institutions that were closed and consolidated with neighboring communities.

Bushy Fork had several schools that were once located in the township, including one of the earliest in the state, the Van Hook School, which was built around 1810 at the intersection of Payne's Tavern Road and Whittown Road. The school made of logs was recently removed to the museum campus and became a permanent exhibit.

Bushy Fork Township was also home to the Bushy Fork School, built in 1907 at Roseville and Hester's Store Road on

Willie Wilkerson's property. In 1936, the "new school" was built near Bushy Fork store and closed in 1969. This was part of a pattern that found student population areas in the county changing, necessitating either the construction of new schools or transfer to a nearby area school.

Churches also played an early part in Bushy Fork's history, and one of the earliest was Wheeler's Primitive Baptist Church. On Saturday, July 3, 1791, the first services were held at Wheeley's Meeting House. This was an arm of Flat River Church, according to the 1792 minutes; it separated in 1792 and was then called the Upper South Hico Church. In 1816, Nathaniel Norfleet of Person County deeded five acres of land on which Wheeley's Meeting House was situated. The name was later changed to Wheeler's, as it is known today. In addition, one of the largest African American churches in the county is Union Grove Baptist Church located in the Bushy Fork Township.

Some of the names common to Bushy Fork Township listed as heads of families circa 1850–1880 are Bradsher, Torian, Whitfield, Foushee, Russell, McMullen, Hurdle, Lee and Baynes.

One of the earliest doctors in Bushy Fork was Raney Curry Baynes, who was born in 1818 and moved into the area as a frontier doctor in the mid-1800s. His son, Ralph Sidney Baynes, followed in his father's footsteps and became a doctor as well. And, like his grandfather and father, Ralph Henry Baynes entered the medical profession and practiced medicine in the Hurdle Mills area.

A Bushy Fork township native son, Robert Lester Blackwell, was the first North Carolinian to receive the Congressional Medal of Honor, given posthumously for his service in World War I. Blackwell was born in Hurdle Mills in 1895, entered the army in 1917 and died in 1918.

In 1932, Bushy Fork resident Onnie Edna Whitfield asked her neighbors and friends for pieces of dress material to make a friendship quilt, which took two years to complete. After the quilt was finished, she asked those same neighbors and friends to sign their squares. Some of those signatures on the quilt include Mrs. Elma Wade, Leasburg; Thelma Lloyd, Durham; Christine Foushee, Roxboro; "Precious" Reade Foushee, Roxboro; O. Dell Allen, Roxboro; Dorene Brooks, Prospect Hill; Fannie Snipes, Roxboro; Beulah Blalock, Roxboro; and Bettie Whitfield, Hurdle Mills.

Person County has eight listings on the National Register of Historic Places. According to its website, the Henry Vernon House, located in the Bushy Fork township, was added to the Register in 1983. The historic significance is the architecture and engineering in the Vernon House's Greek revival, Queen Anne style.

The Bushy Fork Homemakers were first organized in the early 1900s as a Tomato Club, according to the *Courier-Times* Centennial issue. The Tomato Club was organized to help the homemakers can tomatoes. They also made orange marmalade and probably learned to can other fruits and vegetables. If the homemakers canned more tomatoes than they needed, they took them to Raleigh to sell.

The Home Demonstration Club was organized in 1938. The name of the club was changed to Extension Homemakers Club in the late 1960s. More recently, the organization again underwent a name change and became known as the Bushy Fork Extension and Community Association.

Written by Vicki Berry.

Originally appeared in the Courier-Times, *August 18, 2004, sec. B1.*

Centre Grove and Caltolina: Forgotten Villages

A framed 1928 soil map of Person County reveals that there once existed communities, churches, schools and post offices in the Allensville Township that are no longer familiar to its citizens today. Some of those places include the school and post office of Centre Grove, the community of Caltolina (Catalina), Mount Gideon Church and Burma Church. Also detailed on the 1928 map within the Allensville Township are Five Fork School, Lawson's Chapel, St. Paul's Church and Rocky (Rock) Grove.

A few references to the community of Centre Grove can be found in Stuart Wright's 1977 book, *Historical Sketch of Person County*.

At a time when the county prospered commercially, the firm of Allen and Royster was located in Allensville in the 1850s. Day and Townshend, later succeeded by Benjamin A. Thaxton, was located in Centre Grove.

Between the end of the Civil War and 1872, nine tobacco "manufactories" or factories were either newly established or re-established in the county, and at least two of these were in Centre Grove, namely Thomas and Thomas and J.W. Philpot.

Also following the war, flour, corn and saw mills were in operation throughout the county. In Allensville were Reade, Stanford and Moore, who had operations at Centre Grove.

In 1877, there was only one private school in Roxboro. By 1884, three private schools had been established, including a co-educational school at Centre Grove operated by W.H. Royster. Six years later, new schools cropped up throughout the county, including a school at Allensville with J.J. Scarborough as principal.

According to the *NC Guide and Business Office Companion* published in 1877, the Allensville district had two out of the nine post offices in the county at that time. The others listed are Roxboro, Bushy Fork, Cunningham's Store, Hester's Store, Hurdle's Mills, Mount Tirzah and Woodsdale.

Postmasters at the Centre Grove post office, as listed in *Person County Heritage*, were John K. Bumpass, 1856; John T. Townsend, 1857; Elizabeth V. Bumpass, 1866; Sarah Thaxton, 1871; Benjamin F. Thaxton, 1873; C.C. Townsend, 1885; Woodson L. Thomas, 1885; Wm. H. Tilley, 1893; Edwin T. Mooney, 1895; Peter G. Pritchett, 1897. In 1914, the post office was discontinued to Timberlake.

Centre Grove, thirteen miles from Roxboro and located on an 1895 U.S. atlas, was listed with a population of seventy-three and containing a post office but no rail line.

Another sleepy village that once dotted Allensville's rolling-hill landscape is the less documented community called Caltolina, which was named after the Calton family. Unlike its sister community, Caltolina could boast a railway if not a post office. The Calton family owned several acres in the vicinity; however, today a road sign is the only evidence of the former community.

According to Person County history enthusiast Clark Oakley, the prominent family owned a lumber mill and interest in the railroad. The lumber business was the purpose and reason for the tramway that ran to Caltolina farms, Oakley says. At that time, a tramway was a smaller railroad connected to the lumber industry.

"Trees as big around as a Buick were removed from the virgin forest," he says, which was cut for timber. Several million cubic feet of lumber were removed from Caltolina Farms, loaded on the tram and hauled to the main depot.

This tram is also the subject of a tragic story researched and documented by Oakley. The train's last journey from Pick's Siding to Caltolina ended in a catastrophe. The tram exploded, killed two men and injured three others. In 1992, remnants of the tragedy were found when the farm was being surveyed.

R.W. Massie and Co. Tramway ran from the junction on the North and Western Railway to the lumber mills. With the explosion came the demise of the tramway; the company pulled up the track and sold it for scrap.

Written by Vicki Berry.
Partial reprint of an article that originally appeared in the Courier-Times, *March 3, 2004, sec. B1.*

Colonel Dan: "Not Mean, Just a Little Devilish"

It would seem that one of the most colorful characters in Person County history was a Graham native who migrated to Roxboro in the late 1800s. Colonel Dan Andrews (no one knows how he came to be called "Colonel") ran a barroom in uptown Roxboro, sired nine children, purportedly ran a distillery, loved practical jokes and left a legacy that was fondly remembered for decades.

In 1967 the local newspaper reported that, "Old timers say the city limits of Roxboro were constructed so Dan Andrews' distillery would be inside the city limits. The state had a law, they say, that all distilleries had to be inside the city limits." Colonel Dan "reportedly owned a great deal of property and at his death he owned a block of buildings from the present location of Dr. F.E. McFayden's Optometrist Office to Foushee Street."

Justice of the Peace Henry O'Briant remembered Andrews as a practical joker who was "not mean, just a little devilish."

In Colonel Dan's time, the front entrance of the old Thomas and Holeman Hardware Store on Main Street faced the alley and "some say there were steps on Main Street which went down to the barroom. They say the bar was on the right as you went in the front door."

O'Briant said that Andrews "ran a clean barroom. No gunfights, or anything." He operated the barroom from about 1885 to 1890.

According to O'Briant's account in the December 1967 *Courier-Times*, Andrews "used to ride a Winton automobile with a live monkey chained to the radiator. During World War I he was bad about selling people five pounds of salt for five pounds of sugar."

Legend has it Andrews once sold a friend salt for sugar, and the friend's wife was none too happy when her pie turned out a bit on the salty side. When his friend confronted Andrews, he reportedly slapped his knee and vowed he had merely picked up the wrong bag.

Two years later, according to lore, Andrews asked his friend where he might find sweet potato plants. The friend brought Andrews about two hundred plants, which the Colonel planted and cultivated—and which turned out to be morning glories.

Another story has it that Andrews had a prized cherry tree, and someone began stealing his cherries during the night. The Colonel had a good idea who the culprits were and devised a way to catch the three boys he suspected. He told one of the boys that he knew someone was stealing his cherries and asked the boy to help him catch the guilty party.

"There's a full moon tonight," Andrews told the boy, "and I want you to come over and climb up in the top of the cherry tree and wait for the culprit."

Likely the boy thought it would be a good joke on old Dan, the paper reports, since he was the one taking the cherries. He agreed to climb the tree.

The story goes that the boy climbed up to the top of the cherry tree and Colonel Dan loaded his shotgun with peas. He then went out and shot the boy "clean out of the tree." Forever after, the boy was called "Pea Soup."

In June 1915, the *Courier* reported that, "Yesterday afternoon Sheriff Thompson got wind of the coming of two automobiles loaded with corn liquor, and about four o'clock he summoned a posse and put out for the chase."

The blockaders were sighted near the Brooksdale community, and the posse commenced pursuit. But the blockaders were wise to the chase and "made flight, and being in a Hupmobile, which is no mean machine, they made good time." But the "sheriff and his crowd were gaining on them, and when getting within distance began shooting at the machine in an attempt to puncture the tires, but in this they failed, however, they lodged a few bird shot in the arm of one of the blockaders."

When this happened, the two men in the vehicle "left the car and took to the woods." But, given that "Sheriff Thompson proved to be the better sprinter," he ran them down and hauled them in.

While the sheriff was thus occupied, Deputy R.W. Morris was "chasing another machine which had acted suspiciously, and after a lively chase and coming too close the driver of this car drove into the woods and left his car." The car was a Reo, according to the newspaper account, which belonged to a Mr. D.M. Andrews. About sixty gallons of liquor were found in the car.

The newspaper reported that, "This morning Mr. Andrews came in and gave himself up."

He was sentenced to six months in jail and his Reo was auctioned off, with the county buying the car for $280. Colonel

Dan appealed to the governor for a pardon, but after a three-hour hearing in the governor's office, with "seventy-five or more men from Person, Durham and Guilford counties, lead attorneys General B.S. Royster of Oxford and Victor S. Bryant of Durham" appearing in the interest of Andrews, the pardon was denied.

Andrews reportedly told the governor that he was returning from a visit and on the road "encountered a party whose automobile had broken down. One of the men in the car requested that he give them relief to the extent of transporting the ten cases of whiskey which they were carrying some distance down the road and place it in the bushes." Andrews said he complied, but was spotted by the posse, thus waiting "in hiding" while the officers seized the hooch.

The *Courier* reported, "Reverend J.J. Boone of Roxboro opposed the pardon and described Andrews as a stumbling block in the way of moral uplift in Person County. He claimed that ninety percent of the people of Person are in sympathy with the liquor traffic and charged that certain ministers of the county not only are not opposed to it but drink with the church members.

"Reverend M. Warren, who appeared for Andrews, arose to personal privilege on this. He did not wish to be included in the list of drinking preachers."

Colonel Dan returned to Roxboro and served his jail term, but it was said he was allowed to move freely about the town and that most of his meals were cooked and delivered to him by local folks.

Originally appeared in the Courier-Times *Centennial Edition, 1982, sec. C19.*

Miss Molly's Matchmaking

Molly Strum Barrett turned her own personal tragedy into an avenue of happiness for other Personians for nearly forty years.

In 1926, after her husband of just three months died, leaving her pregnant, she moved from the Allensville community to town in Roxboro and opened Miss Molly's Boarding House. Young single women who came to town as schoolteachers, secretaries, church workers and the like had a safe place to stay that offered them not only a place to sleep, but also an education in how to be proper ladies. The young women also often found themselves the object of Miss Molly's matchmaking.

Mrs. Jean Newell, who today works as docent and exhibits coordinator at the Person County Museum of History, was one of Miss Molly's boarders—and a benefactor of her matchmaking.

Mrs. Newell recalls how Miss Molly raised her son, George, alone, and sent him to Wake Forest University, after which he became a radiologist.

"George and Miss Molly were matchmakers," Newell recalls with a smile. "If you stayed at the house, you got the benefit of being matched up with somebody." Newell found her husband, Henry, through the Barretts' efforts. But, Newell recalls, one had to always act like a lady if one stayed under Miss Molly's roof. She was strict about the gentlemen callers staying in the parlor and going nowhere else in the house, especially nowhere near the girls' rooms.

"You had to be ladylike," Newell says, "and very careful about the boys staying in the parlor."

She recalls Miss Molly as "a teeny little thing," very proper for the most part. But what many didn't know was that Miss Molly had a "wooden leg." Newell said Miss Molly would never tell how she lost the leg, but after supper, she would go into her room and take off the wooden leg and "hang it on the bedpost." Miss Molly would then proceed to "hop around on one leg" if she had to move around anymore at night.

Miss Molly's boarding house was on Morgan Street in Roxboro for six years. In 1932, she built a new house and moved her charges to the corner of Reams and Morgan, where she would remain until the close of the boarding house on December 15, 1963.

In January 1963, W.F. "Bill" Timberlake wrote in the *Courier-Times*, "With the closing of the year 1962, Roxboro is losing a very famous guest home that has been operated on the corner of Reams Avenue and Morgan Street for more than three decades."

Timberlake went on to write, "With a physical handicap, Miss Molly not only looked after and operated her home with many guests but she raised her son, Dr. George Barrett, and her niece Mrs. Terry. During the period of this operation she has had several periods of illness and accidents, but with a determination that was remarkable she attended to her work even if she had to use crutches or a wheelchair to get around."

According to the *Courier-Times* article noting the closing of Miss Molly's, she was a woman of unusual ability, hospitality and warmth. She had an uncanny knack for selecting "satisfactory guests for her home," and "anyone who has not had an opportunity to eat one of her delicious meals has indeed missed a treat."

Miss Molly did not like to have her establishment referred to as a rooming house or boarding house and never allowed her home to be referred to as such. Her clientele were guests, plain and simple. And, as Mrs. Newell can attest and the newspaper noted, "The ground work for many a romance was laid around the table in Miss Molly's dining room and living room. There are many couples that are now living in Roxboro and the vicinity that can attest to this fact."

Aside from caring for her guests and her matchmaking activities, Miss Molly was active in the community. She helped organize the Women's Hospital Auxiliary and helped bring Roxboro its first hospital, Person County Memorial, in 1950.

She was named "Person County Mother of the Year" in 1956, and the newspaper said that this was "a most deserving tribute."

Written by Phyliss Boatwright.

Sources: The Courier-Times Centennial Edition, *1982, sec. G11;*

Mrs. Jean Newell; Person County Museum of History exhibit.

Hurdle Mills: And Then There Was One

At one time, mills not only dotted the landscape of Person County, but were also situated in and close to communities of all sizes throughout colonial America.

Milling played an instrumental part in the development of rural communities. Typically, once a mill prospered, it was surrounded by a small community.

A mill or milling operation can be described as the process of converting raw materials into a manufactured product. Those raw materials can be wood converted to paper, cotton converted to fabric, or corn or wheat ground into meal or flour.

Communities sprung up in America's countryside due to mills, and frequently the new villages took on the name of the mill and owner.

As America grew, so did the number and various types of mills, as evidenced by the number of towns that contain the word "mill" in the name, although the mill has long ceased operating within the

community. North Carolina boasts a number of towns named after mills including Mills River, Concord Mills, Clarks Mills, Union Mills, Hope Mill, Mill Spring and South Mills, to name a few.

Evidence of two such mill towns in Person County can still easily be found on county maps. One is the village of Hurdle Mills, which prides itself on containing one of Person County's three town post offices. The other mill town is McGehees Mill, which is now familiar to most northern county newcomers due to the road of the same name.

Yet other mills and perhaps mill villages, though they are not so easily found on maps, are remembered by folks who have lived in and have had ancestors who spoke of the small mill communities, such as Bartons Mill in Timberlake, Woodsdale Mill and Bushy Fork Mill.

And still evidence remains of long-forgotten mills. Folks often speak of happening across remnants of a mill of some sort while walking or hunting in the woods.

Today's solitary Person County mill and lone reminder of the important community gristmill is Hurdle's Mill. Though currently a feed mill, it can trace its early beginnings in the form of a flour gristmill, according to Michael Dixon, who along with his father, Jasper "Tink" Dixon, own and operate Hurdle's Mill.

William Daniel built the original building in 1846. A rock and wooden dam was built across the Flat River to furnish power to operate the corn and wheat mill. During the Civil War, the building was burned, and all that remained of the razed mill was the foundation, explains Dixon. About 1890, the foundation was reused to become the base for a new structure, which remains standing and in use today. Not only has the building of the mill changed and been added to over the years, but the names of both the mill and the town have changed as well.

The nineteenth-century small mill town became known as Daniels Mill, after the owner and operator of the mill, William Daniel, an ancestor of the current Daniel family of Hurdle Mills, according to documentation collected by Dorothy Carver of Roxboro. Carver, the daughter of Jasper Dixon Sr., has collected considerable information on the village of Hurdle Mills and the mill, which she has compiled in a notebook.

After William Daniel died, the mill passed into the hands of the Hurdle family, and subsequently the name of the community was changed to Hurdle's Mill in 1859, then to Hurdle Mills in 1892. The mill changed hands a few times until Jasper A. Dixon Sr. bought the establishment in 1928.

Current mill manager Dixon said his grandfather was not a newcomer to milling operations when he bought the mill from Mark Garrett in the 1920s; he also owned a mill in the community of Woodsdale.

At the time of the purchase by J.A. Dixon Sr., the site consisted of a miller's compound, miller's cabin, smokehouse, chicken coop and stable. A one-lane bridge was also located on the site, along with a blacksmith shop. In addition to managing Hurdle's Mill, the current operator's grandfather also purchased the village blacksmith shop, running the shop in partnership with Cyrus White.

The site contained about thirty-five acres, which included the millpond, as the mill was water wheel driven. Water was

a necessary component of the mill operation, so the mill was situated on the bank of the Flat River. Water from the river ran into a reservoir, called the millpond. From the pond, the water flowed through a millrace to rotate the wheel, which in turn provided the power to operate the mill. Now the millpond is no longer necessary.

The portion of the river where the mill was built had a partial dam naturally formed by a sizeable boulder. The milldam burst in the early 1920s near the site of the big rock. According to Carver, after the fall of the dam the mill was run by machinery.

The large rock also caused a "swimming hole" to form in the river. Dixon recalls playing and swimming "at the rock" as a child, as did many of the neighborhood children.

That was back when communities were more close-knit and were more self-contained, said Dixon. Hurdle Mills had its own school where children attended school from first grade through high school. The school closed its doors after the 1962–63 school year. Now the community school, like many others in the county, is home to a county recreation department park or ball field. While Hurdle Mills may have lost its school due to progress, it still contains a post office, country store, market, café and a few other commercial establishments in addition to the mill.

Currently decorating the interior of the building are artifacts of the mill's bygone years, such as a simple, uncomplicated scale, a hand-pumped fire extinguisher and a wooden grain auger. The auger was used to move flour along its course. The homemade wooden spout hanging on the wall was used when the mill ran elevators, which, at that time, was a series of cups attached on a belt that would convey corn or grain to the top of the mill.

Just as the equipment, names and owners have changed over the years, the nature of the operation of Hurdle's Mill has also changed. Most of the feeds manufactured at the mill today are textured or mash feeds, made from grains brought in primarily from the Shenandoah Valley, for horse, cattle, chicken, hog, sheep, llama and goat. The mill operator and nine employees also retail feed for dogs, cats, parakeet and ostriches. The modern mill has also changed and expanded to include items for the lawn and garden.

While time has mandated modifications to mills and mill villages, one aspect that time has not altered is that mice like to make grain mills their home. And naturally, mill owners have combated the troublesome pest with the mouse's number one domesticated enemy: the cat. Dixon said that as long as he can remember there have been cats at the mill. He recalls that when he was a kid his grandfather, who was by then perhaps eighty years old, continued to make the trek to the mill every day in order to feed the cats. Today's visitors to the mill can still catch a glimpse of the vermin-ridding feline snoozing in the sunlight atop a sack of feed just as the scene would have appeared one hundred years ago.

Written by Vicki Berry.

Originally appeared in the Courier-Times, *May 24, 2003, sec. B1.*

Honestest and Bravest

The Sappony, known during the last century as the Indians of Person County, played an important part in the early settlement of the area. It was members of this Indian tribe who helped William Byrd establish the boundary line between Virginia and North Carolina. The same boundary passes through the heart of the community. Byrd's journal refers to the Sappony as the "honestest and bravest" Indians.

For centuries, the tribal members of the Sappony have called home the area referred to as the High Plains Indian community. The historic community is located between the area formed by the waters of Hyco-o-tee, the Siouan word for turkey buzzard roost, which was later shortened to Hyco River; Sugar Tree Creek, later changed to Mayo Creek; and Blew Wing Creek.

The tribe's insignia is representative of its history. The seven feathers tied together at the base of the insignia symbolize the seven families that make up the Sappony tribe. The feathers are tied together to represent the close-knit community. The crops featured prominently in the center symbolize the role tobacco and other crops play in the tribe's economy and in allowing the community to remain together. The three arrowheads in the insignia represent the tribal identity as Sappony people and the stars symbolize the important role faith occupies in the community.

An exhibit housed in the Person County Museum of History called the "Honestest and Bravest" summarizes the tribe's history from first contact. Much of the story of the community is told through maps and copies of original documents. "The maps tell where we are and where we have been," says Dante Desiderio, tribal director. The first and earliest map is one of John Smith's. It is interesting to note that it is in German and drawn from the viewpoint of a ship: north is indicated on the right-hand side.

Many of the known tribes in 1612 are indicated on the map. This was the first time that the Monasusapanough, later shortened to Sappony, were shown on a map.

Another map from 1671, completed by early explorer John Lederer, documents villages and "shows us near where we are now, and at this point we have already become involved in trading," says Desiderio.

There is awcopy taken from Jefferson's library of a signed treaty showing two signatories, the chief of state and the king of war of the tribe. The signatures indicate that the Indians were learning English at this time.

It was at this point that a turn of events took place. While Berkeley was governor of Virginia, there were good relations, but when the Ochenekee massacre occurred under the vigilante Nathaniel Bacon, the Indians moved out of Virginia and into North Carolina, where they stayed until the eighteenth century.

Trade was very important. Everything was based on trade, and when the Sappony moved from Virginia it left a vacuum in commerce. When Spotswood became governor attempts were made to get the Sappony back, not only for trade but for

The tribal insignia of the Sappony.

protection as well. There was not a single attack in the settlements by foreign Indians while the Sappony were guarding the frontier.

In 1708, the tribe moved to Fort Christanna on the south side of Virginia. The fort was part of the grand plan of Spotswood in his attempts to increase trade in Virginia.

The fort was large and built to be self-sufficient. Sappony lived in and around the fort. The stay at the fort was brief but important as the first Indian school was established, Christianity was learned and the Indians continued the trade by working as middlemen.

The fort closed in 1718; however, Sappony remained in the area. Trade continued and the Sappony moved and lived along the trading paths. "Just like trade is the source of our family names, trade also dictated where we lived and the reason we moved," says Desiderio.

The seven family names of Stewart, Epps, Shepherd, Martin, Johnson, Talley and Coleman can be linked with early traders and explorers in the area.

The High Plains School represents a unique history in itself as possibly the only Indian school to be funded by two states. In 1911 North Carolina recognized and funded the High Plains School, and for two years the Virginia residents were not allowed to attend. At last, arrangements were made with Virginia and North Carolina in that both states would provide education for the community. The community provided the land and school, and the states provided the teachers.

The community is bound together by the value placed on the church and education with the Indian church at the center of the community, according to Desiderio. "And we remain a very close-knit community today," says Tribal Chief Otis Martin.

"We would like to offer tribal members more opportunities for education and economic development and better serve our members' needs," Desiderio says. "We are proud of the work we have completed in the past—it has been an interesting journey."

Written by Dante Desiderio.

Partial reprint of an article that originally appeared in the Courier-Times.

The Sappony: Written and Oral Histories

Written History

The tobacco featured in the center of our tribal insignia has meaning far greater than the crop grown for smoking or used as snuff. As Indians, and as community members of High Plains, tobacco holds a special place among the crops given to us for our sustenance.

Before the Sappony settled in High Plains, tobacco held a central role in our spiritual sustenance. Prior to a hunt, a sprinkling of tobacco was offered in return for a safe journey and a good hunt. Prior to entering into battle, tobacco was offered in return for courage and honor. And in ceremonies, tobacco and its smoke were used as a gift and as a way to communicate.

While in High Plains, tobacco took on a different but equally important role for the Sappony. As the center of the High Plains

economy, tobacco allowed the Sappony to remain together, build community churches and schools and help one another out in times of need.

The self-sufficiency that tobacco allowed was especially important for a number of reasons. In the early part of the nineteenth century, Indians were not welcome or wanted in North Carolina and Virginia, as evidenced by the Cherokee removal in the western part of North Carolina. Staying together and keeping to themselves was a matter of survival, and the livelihood gained from farming tobacco allowed the Sappony to remain together and remain in their homelands. In addition, Indians in High Plains found it difficult to find work outside of farming in the community. A few worked at the sawmill or worked for the railroad when it came through High Plains, but the community members of High Plains frequently found themselves unable to secure good paying jobs because of their status as Indians. Often, the jobs they did receive were marginal at best, and when a white person wanted the same job, the Indians found themselves wanting for work.

Some in High Plains decided to take their chances when the railroad came through and go north to find work. A number of families settled into the region of southeastern Pennsylvania and began careers they could only dream about at home. Today, many families with strong ties to the community of High Plains are still found in the southeast corner of Pennsylvania.

Written by Dante Desiderio.

ORAL HISTORY

Lois Epps Jones was one of those Sappony living in High Plains who chose to leave the community to find other opportunities. Her story, called "Zan Epps' Daughter," was recorded by David Cecelski as part of the Southern Oral History Program. It was later published in the April 11, 1999 edition of the *Raleigh News & Observer*.

Jones left High Plains to become a nurse in the army only to return to her roots in High Plains. Her father, Alexander Epps, was one of the tobacco farmers in the community.

> *I used to love sitting outside when my dad was curing tobacco. We would sit out in the moonlight and roast apples, and he'd tell me about the things that happened when he was growing up. Naturally, when we were working in the tobacco, we didn't have all the modern things. My dad never had a tractor; never had a chain saw. We were what you called the dirt farmers. We had two little mules. Those old mules were so mean that they would*

practically eat you up alive. They would have you as ragged as a jaybird.

We Indians lived separate and apart. We were set aside because of the color of our skin. We could not go out and eat a meal in public. We could not go in the restaurants because they only had white and colored. We weren't colored. We weren't white. We were neither. Blacks at least had a section at the theater; there was no place for us. If we needed to go to the bathroom, right up on the door: white, colored, but no Indian. And for me, as an Indian, to speak to you! Not on your life! We had our own church, our own school. We'd go to Roxboro maybe once a year if we were going in after a pair of shoes. We never had any use for the law. We weren't calling the police, and the police wasn't coming.

Growing up at the farm, we didn't have time to get out into other things. We were too busy trying to make a living. Mom couldn't have taken care of ten children if everybody didn't have a job. We didn't have running water. We had to carry water from the old spring. In the afternoons, if she was going to wash tomorrow, we would bring water up, store it in tubs and a barrel the day before. In the summer, when we were out of school, we would take all the clothes down to the branch and wash there. We'd dip our water out, make us a fire in the pot and heat our water.

By the time you did all that, and take care of your cows, your horses, your pigs, your chickens, you didn't have a lot of time to think about entertainment. You were so glad to get finished. [Health] problems then! There was nobody going to the gym and all that, because the gym was right there! All we were looking for was a place to lay down, quietly. We didn't have to have a book accompany us to bed to drop off to sleep!

We were brought up in church, believing in the way of life that the Bible taught. Never a day started that my parents didn't ask God's protection for us and them. It was instilled in us to know that as we lived, so would we die. You don't live alone, and you don't die alone. I was taught that how I live my life has an effect not only on me, but on the rest of my family. If you and your wife work in public, your child will never have the connection with you that we had with our parents, daddy being a farmer. We were taught things. We were around them. If I had a problem, I didn't go to my peers or call the school counselor. My counselor was my mom. I was born in the warmth of her bed. I remember back, as a very, very young child, standing between my dad's knees in front of the fireplace where it was warm, and my baby brother laying in my mom's lap. He used to pretend to cry in the evenings, and she would sit him down in her apron and pull off his little shoes and he would warm his feet by that fire. This bonding is what he wanted.

Poor nothing! No child could have been happier. You see, I didn't realize how disadvantaged I was because I had so much of the things that are essential. I had love. I had security. I had encouragement. You never had to worry in High Plains, because we were all for one and one for all. Nobody had to fear each other. My sisters and I would get on the road and walk to Bethel Hill on a Saturday, to Virgilina, to Mayo. We'd walk miles and miles. And we had so much joy in our lives, that the tragedies became so much smaller.

I would have preferred to stay, but I knew I couldn't. If I could have lived right here in Person County and taught school at Bethel Hill or Roxboro, that would have been different. But I couldn't, not as an Indian. I knew if I ever were to accomplish anything, I had to leave to do it.

I was the first High Plains girl that ever went away from home that wasn't married and moved with a husband. My parents knew how much I wanted something for myself, but others laughed at me. Yes, I was the laughing stock! The dreamer! "Your daddy doesn't even make his expenses," they'd say. "He can't ever finance you to do the things you're dreaming about." I didn't expect him to! But one day I was going to grow up. I was determined.

I felt there had to be somewhere in this world I wasn't going to be treated any different because of who I was and where I came from. When they asked, "Who are your parents? Where do you come from?" there had to be somewhere that it didn't make any difference when I said, "I'm Zan Epps' daughter. I'm an Indian from Person County."

I wasn't ashamed of being Zan Epps' daughter. I was proud. I had one of the greatest dads. Daddy didn't go to college. He couldn't read or write, but he was one of the wisest guys I've met. Education is from a book. Wisdom is from God. Any guy could take two little fuzzy mules and this land, raise ten children and a sickly wife and never take a loaf of bread as a handout, to me he's not an ignorant guy. He was uneducated in a lot of things, but life didn't happen to be one of them.

And let me tell you: if you could have seen that old man's face the first time when I came home from the army! When I stepped off that train, oh, the look on his face! The pride, the joy. Words cannot express it. Somebody said to him, "Who are you looking for?" And my daddy raised his hand, proud as a peacock, and said, "That's my daughter."

Lois Jones has made her home on Epps-Martin Road directly across from her father's house. Her son, Larry Jones, works for the state of North Carolina and is involved in helping Indian communities across the state through his seat on the North Carolina Indian Housing Authority.

Sapon the Warrior

The Susquesahanaugh, or Susquehanna as they are called today, were known by their symbol of a terrapin, which characterized the tribe known for its wisdom. The Akenatzy or the Occaneechi were known by the symbol of a serpent, which characterized the tribes known for their wrath. The Sappony were given the symbol of three arrows. The symbol of three arrows characterized the Sappony as a tribe known for its warriors and hunters. Today, three arrowheads, prominently displayed on the tribal insignia beneath the seven stars, represent the symbol of the three arrows. The arrowheads represent the tribe's identity and character as Sappony people.

The symbol of three arrows was used when the Sappony were trading among the colonial settlements. Three arrows were tattooed on the shoulder of the Sappony and later placed on a copper medallion worn around their necks. These symbols would allow the colonists to easily identify the tribal affiliation of an approaching Indian. Since the Sappony were a key part of southwestern colonial and Indian trade during the latter part of the seventeenth century and the first half of the eighteenth century, these symbols were probably easily recognized and commonplace for the Indians, traders and settlers.

How did the Sappony earn their warrior status? A story has survived among the Siouan tribes about one of the Sappony warriors who was respected and honored by both colonial frontiersman and other tribes from New York to South Carolina. The name of the warrior was Sapon.

Sapon was hunting alone in the woods one day. While he was hunting, he wandered upon a party of Seneca Indians, or Sinnagars, as the Sappony called them. Since the Sinnagars were the centuries-old enemies of the Sappony, Sapon wisely ran to take cover behind a rock. But while he was running, one of the Sinnagars spotted him.

Sapon was very fast and skilled at shooting, but nonetheless, while he ran for cover toward home, the enemy caught up to him. A fierce battle ensued, during which he killed seven of the Sinnagars before the rest of the party surrounded him and took him captive.

The Sinnagars paused to bury their fellow warriors and carried Sapon off to their country, which was in New York. Even though the Sinnagars were saddened and felt shamed that one warrior was able to kill seven of their men, they treated him with respect since they, like other tribes, saw it as a great virtue to be a good warrior. If Sapon had acted as a coward, they would have had no respect for him and would have killed him rather than take him as a captive.

The Sinnagars, with Sapon in tow, reached their country, and when they carried him through several of their towns, the women and children lined up to form a gauntlet and beat and whipped him according to their laws of justice. Finally, he was condemned to be executed by fire.

Sapon had been through a great ordeal. He had hardly eaten for days, he was marched for days to New York as a captive, he

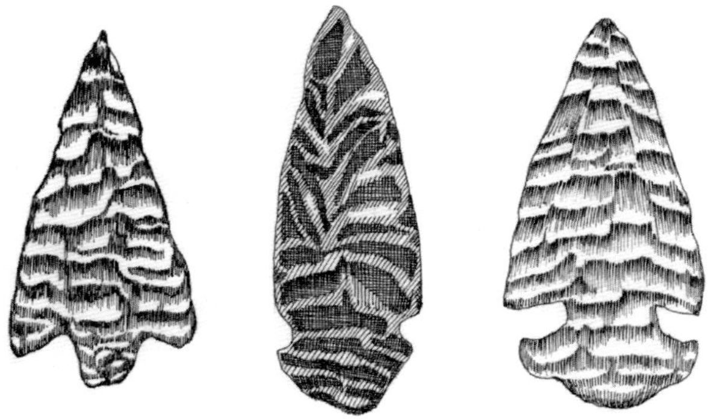

had slept on the bare ground with barely enough clothes to cover his body, his arms and legs were spread apart with ropes as he was beaten and whipped in several towns. An Englishman who told the story centuries ago said, "The majority of English would pass out and welcome the end of this torture," but he said he never knew this to be the case with Indian warriors.

Sapon was no exception. He remained cool-headed and brave, while acting the part of a weak and beaten warrior so well that he fooled his captors, who thought he had no energy or fight left in him.

The Sinnagars took Sapon unbound down to the river, toward his execution. A parade of Sinnagars gathered to see the execution of the great warrior who took the lives of seven of their men. In a sudden burst, Sapon ran down several Sinnagars standing in his way and sprung off into the river.

He swam under the water like an otter and only took a breath when he reached the opposite side. He climbed up the river bank, and even though he had every reason to keep running as fast as he could, since some of the Sinnagars were in the water after him and others were shooting their guns in his direction, he stopped. His heart did not allow him to go on without thanking the Seneca for their "favors," so in defiance he turned his backside to the Seneca, slapped it, moved it around, put up a war whoop as a defiant salute and darted off into the woods with the Seneca chasing after him.

It was midnight when Sapon stopped running and finally rested. He rested for two days when he discovered some of his pursuers—five Sinnagar Indians—in a camp. He hid and waited. He thought of all he had been through and how he was tired, naked, torn and hungry. He thought about how the Seneca would not let him rest until they captured him or killed him. He waited until all were asleep.

Then, he crept toward them in silence, took one of their tomahawks and fought and killed all five Sinnagars. He took their scalps, a fine gun, ammunition and provisions. He clothed himself, ate and set out for home. He didn't sleep for several more nights until he came across the place where he had been captured and where he killed seven of the Sinnagar warriors. He dug up the warriors and took their scalps so that he could get rest from the warrior's spirits in this world and so the warriors would rest in the next. He continued toward home.

Other Sinnagar parties who were in pursuit came across the camp where their fellow warriors did battle with Sapon. They saw some of their bravest warriors laying there defeated in battle. It gave them a great shock. They decided to turn back in retreat, figuring that if Sapon could do that much damage when he was naked, beaten, held captive and unarmed, then what could he do with arms, food and rest. If they continued in their pursuit, their fate would be the same as their fellow warriors since they concluded Sapon was a warrior of supernatural status.

The story of Sapon has survived over hundreds of years as a testament to his character as a warrior and to the character of his people. The three arrowheads on the Sappony insignia symbolize the character of the Sappony people as great hunters and warriors. The arms and adversaries may have changed but the Sappony character remains.

Written by Dante Desiderio.

Sappony Faith: The Tie That Binds

For well over two hundred years, faith has been the sustenance that has kept the seven main families together in High Plains. The seven stars that rise above the other symbols on the tribal insignia represent this faith.

While in High Plains, the Sappony families first attended Bethel Hill Baptist Church. The earliest minutes of the church reflect community members being received and baptized. Some, like Allen Epps, were recorded as early as 1801. Later entries record other families like the Colemans, Stewarts, Shepherds, Talleys and Martins.

Bethel Hill originally had blacks, whites and Indians all attending church together. While they may have attended the same church together, they did not sit or mix together. The whites occupied the main seating area on the lower level, the free blacks had a separate section, the slaves were placed outside and the Indians sat apart from both. This relationship became strained during Nat Turner's rebellion. Panic spread throughout white communities in North Carolina and Virginia. The areas around Roxboro in North Carolina and South Boston in Virginia were no exception. Churches, including Bethel Hill, began to separate along the lines of whites and everyone else. There was a great deal of hysteria in the white ruling class followed by distrust of free blacks and Indians.

The free blacks in the area eventually formed two other churches as a result of the separation in Bethel Hill, one of which became Blue Wing Baptist. The Sappony Indians who attended Bethel Hill remained a part of the congregation but no longer worshiped at the church. Instead they met at what became known as the Epps Meeting House. This was Colonel William Epps's house located along Mayo Creek in High Plains.

Colonel William Epps was the cousin of Allen Epps recorded early in the Bethel Hill minutes. Colonel William Epps was not in the military. His name is derived from the Indian tradition of using military titles to designate a high status within a tribe. Although Colonel William Epps never served in the military, his father, also named William, did. He served in the Revolutionary War with Washington and Lafayette and his fellow Sappony warrior, Thomas Stewart. Both men were granted pensions for their service in the war, which allowed them to secure land in High Plains where their descendants still reside.

The arms-length arrangement between the Sappony and the Bethel Hill church lasted until around 1850, when the Indians in the community decided to worship on their own. Meetings were held in various homes that turned into houses of worship on Sundays. Some in the community remember being told of their grandparents riding buggies or horses to church and looking forward to Sundays when people got to socialize with everybody in the community.

Finally, in 1878, the community was able to build their own church. The new church was called Christ Church at Mayo, and although it was located on the same creek as the Epps Meeting House, it was further downstream, placing it on the Virginia side of High Plains. This church was built by the community on lands donated by community members. There was a provision in the land deed when it was donated that a room be reserved for the education of the children in the community, and the church also became the first school in the community.

The Christ Church at Mayo was replaced by Calvary Baptist Church, but for sixty-eight years it held great memories and served many purposes, not the least of which was having a permanent place to come together for worship and fellowship. Tribal members still remember riding to church in the back of a wagon with their brothers, sisters and other relatives they picked up on the way. During the winter, quilts were piled high to keep the snow off and ward away the chill during the wagon ride to church.

Members recall that a man in the community became the "water boy" for the day. His job was to go down the hill to the spring for water for the preacher before the service. In cold weather, someone from the community headed to the church early on Sunday mornings to start a fire in the woodstove in order to heat up the building before church began. Other members were in charge of cleaning the church.

Since there was no running water, there were no bathrooms. The "facilities" were outside, back in the woods. One side of the woods was reserved for the gentlemen, and another side was reserved for the ladies. As fall came and leaves fell, one needed to head further back into the woods or find a big tree!

Most elder members fondly recall the time after the service ended. The community had a chance to socialize. They looked forward to a long afternoon of picnic lunches on blankets spread over the church grounds. Everyone ate and talked, catching up with friends, cousins, neighbors, aunts and uncles. The children would play for hours, and then late in the afternoon or early evening, everybody loaded up their wagons and headed for home.

In the mid-1940s, the community once again built a church. This time the land and church were placed back in North Carolina along High Plains Road, the main road running through the High Plains community. Calvary Baptist Church is still used today and known as the Indian church. A fellowship hall finished around 1972 allowed members to attend church and gather to fellowship. Calvary stands as a testament to the community's faith while in High Plains for over two hundred years. The descendants of Allen Epps, William Epps and the Stewarts, Colemans, Talleys, Shepherds and Martins listed in the early Bethel Hill minutes can be found in the cemetery behind Calvary and in the pews of Calvary on any given Sunday.

Today members gather from near and far to attend Homecoming. Homecoming is an event that started with the beginning of the Indian church. At Mayo Chapel, as now, Homecoming was the big event, held in the fall of the year at the church. "Dinner on the grounds" was the culmination of a revival. After the Sunday service, everybody shares in "dinner on the grounds," which is a big spread of home-cooked foods laid out on the permanent tables under the trees on the church grounds. Homecoming gives Sappony tribal members, especially those who have moved away, the opportunity to come together, visit and strengthen family ties.

Written by Dante Desiderio.

The Barnett Boys: Little People Who Were Big on Life and Love

It is a Personian's likeness one sees in advertisements for Buster Brown shoes. That's right, the cute "kid" cuddling with Tige the dog is none other than Jack Barnett, one of the "Barnett Boys" of Roxboro, who were known during their lifetimes as the Roxboro dwarves.

Jack, born in 1891, and his younger brother Herbert, who came along in 1898, were the sons of Mary Susan and Samuel Currie Barnett. According to family history available at the Person County Museum of History, both boys were "normal size at birth. Jack was born February 22, 1891, and weighed seven pounds. Herbert was born September 20, 1898," and weighed "seven-and-a-half pounds." The Barnett boys had two brothers, Bryan and Crisp, who were "normal sized," according to family history. There were also two girls born to Mary Susan and Samuel, Mamie Graham and Eva Pearl, both of whom died in childhood.

According to the information at the museum, both Jack and Herbert grew "normally for many years." But when Herbert was seventeen years old, he was just twenty-four inches tall. At twenty-one, Jack was thirty-nine inches tall. Jack would grow to forty-two inches before he stopped adding height, and Herbert would reach the height of thirty-four inches in adulthood.

Jack, whose family history says he had a "name all most bigger than he was," was christened John Winfred Currie Barnett. His brother's full name was Herbert Tyree Barnett.

Both boys attended the John C. Terrell School, located behind Oak Grove Church in the Ceffo Community north of Roxboro.

At age eighteen, Jack left Person County to join the Ringling Brothers, Barnum and Bailey Circus. Nine years later, Herbert joined his brother and the two traveled with the circus, along with their father, for twenty years. The boys' father went along to act as guardian of his sons, and their mother made their costumes.

In the circus, the Barnett boys were known as Captain Jack and his son Herb. According to family history, they "usually were sideshow artists. Most of the time they were billed as father and son."

It is said the Barnett boys made good money but didn't know quite how to handle it. The family history says the boys "were always buying things for their mother. They were very close to her." In fact, according to the information at the museum, "Jack once melted a twenty dollar gold piece into a ring engraved to his mom from Jack."

The story continues that Herbert, while visiting his brother Bryant, noticed a little girl named Margaret Dixon "playing across the street with no shoes on and immediately took her uptown and bought her a pair of shoes."

Family lore has it that Jack and Herbert "were always blessed with good humor. Once a lady at a circus asked, 'Have you always been small?' Jack answered, 'No, I used to be big but I got married and settled down.'"

Jack married a five-foot eight-inch-tall showgirl while he was with Barnum and Bailey. Dorothy Warfield was in the chorus line, according to family history, and hailed from St. Louis, Missouri.

When the couple bought their marriage license, Jack had to be lifted onto a stool in order to be at eye level with his bride.

The couple had a son, Jack Jr., who family history states "was normal sized." According to Mrs. Jean Newell, museum docent, Jack Jr. was almost six feet tall. After his mother returned to performing, Jack Jr. spent much of his time in Roxboro with his grandparents.

Herbert never married, family history has it, "but was always seen in the company of young ladies wherever he went. Once Herbert was seen with a car load of beautiful girls and was seen later that day stopped at a field of violets" so that his lady friends could pick their own bouquets.

Following their stint with the circus, Jack and Herbert got involved in vaudeville. They appeared in "The Little Man's Club," a part of their act in which they dressed "in full formal attire," according to the family history. It is also reported that the brothers had "a spicy dialogue."

Herbert was also known to dress as a woman for a portion of the Barnett brothers' act. He would run from stage, dressed in his formal attire, to reappear as a "young lady in evening dress and a blonde wig." He and his brother would then dance together and "no one suspected it was only two, not three" actors "in the skit." But when the curtain was about to fall, Herbert would remove his wig and bow to the audience.

The brothers Barnett also appeared on Broadway, it is reported, with Herbert playing the role of "Little Nellie Kelly" in 1923. He also played in the movie *Some Baby*.

After the boys left the limelight of stage and screen, Jack took the job as mascot for the Buster Brown shoe company. He was forced to quit this job, however, when he couldn't get along with Tige the dog. So, he returned to Roxboro and worked at a filling station on the corner of Reams Avenue and Morgan Street.

Herbert took a job with J.B. Leathers Tobacco Company, according to family history, where he acted as spokesman and later as "the Meditation Kid."

The brothers also marketed their own brand of cigars, known as Herb and Jack.

Roxboro was proud of the Barnett boys, according to museum information. For years, many folks shared tales about Jack and Herbert. The boys' generosity and wit were often remembered.

The story goes that Herbert loved a good practical joke and once fell on the floor laughing after frightening a clerk in an uptown insurance firm. Legend has it that Mayme Love Barnett was working in the old Thompson Agency one day, behind a big marble counter, when she suddenly heard a voice yell, "Give me your money—this is a stick-up!" She couldn't see anyone, of course, over the large counter and was in such a panic that Herbert couldn't help himself and "literally fell on the floor laughing."

Folks in Roxboro also remembered, for years, seeing Herbert walk the streets uptown using his gold-filled cane and wearing a diamond ring on his finger while calling out a cheery greeting to everyone he met.

As full of life as he was, however, Herbert's time on earth was short. He died suddenly in July 1933 on the return trip from Danville, Virginia, after a night out with friends. According to family history, Herbert was driving but "grew tired and asked James [Carver] to take over." Herbert laid his head in his friend's lap as James drove home. When the group arrived in Roxboro, they were shocked to discover that their friend had died of a heart attack.

Herbert's brother Jack died three years later, in September 1936, after a day of hunting. He was found dead of a heart attack on a friend's porch. Both Barnett boys are buried in the Roxboro Cemetery.

Written by Phyllis Boatwright.

Sources: Mrs. Jean Newell; Person County Museum of History.

The Beams and Bethel Hill

The year was 1886 and the community of Bethel Hill prepared to welcome its new minister, a twenty-nine-year-old native of Cleveland County. Knowing firsthand the difficulties involved in obtaining an education, the Reverend John Alexander Beam determined to combine the two fields of ministry and teaching.

He began by buying the old Flat River Academy, a two-room building that was closed at the time, for a total of one hundred dollars. The building was renamed the Bethel Hill Institute, a name to become synonymous with the instructor himself.

A young Baptist minister who graduated from Wake Forest University in 1885, Beam's foremost objective was to educate and train young men for the ministry. It was only a matter of time before the doors of Bethel Hill Institute were opened to both boys and girls desiring an education.

Reverend Beam advised potential students through various newspapers, "If you want an education, come to Bethel Hill. If you have no money, come anyway." Needless to say, the students came.

The initial two-room building eventually gave way to a "splendid building of goodly proportions and architectural beauty." It is said that the new building opened with the following assets: a mortgage on the Beam home, five dollars in funds, the good will of the Bethel Hill community and faith.

The land for the Institute was donated by Stephen Gentry. Many of Reverend Beam's young male students pledged their support by donating their labor to cut logs and take them to the sawmill. The sawmill owners cooperated by donating the lumber for the school.

Students came from Virginia, South Carolina and Kentucky and soon enrollment grew, along with about twenty-five people who stayed in the Beams' boarding house. According to *Bethel Hill School 1999–2000*, the "Institute was private, but the doors of Reverend and Mrs. Beam's home were never closed to any person who showed the will and determination to work for an education."

The name of the Reverend J.A. Beam was long synonymous with education in Person County but his wife, Mollie Lucas Beam, also was an important figure in the county's history.

A native of South Carolina, Mrs. Beam attended Oxford College in Granville County and came to Person County to teach music at the Bethel Hill Institute, which the Reverend Beam operated. The following September, in 1889, the principal and his new music teacher were married, and the two would spend the remainder of their lives working in education, mainly in Person County.

The Bethel Hill Institute trained young ministers. It was destroyed by fire in 1905, and the Beams left Person County for Danville, Virginia, where the Reverend Beam served as business manager at Averett College and Mrs. Beam taught mathematics and history. The couple also spent time teaching in Prestonburg, Kentucky, before returning to Person County in 1912, at which time Mrs. Beam became principal of the new Bethel Hill High School, one of the first rural schools in the state, built on the site of the former Bethel Hill Institute. The Reverend Beam was named superintendent of schools for Person County.

Mrs. Beam would soon make history by becoming the first woman school superintendent in North Carolina, a post she held from 1923 to 1925, after her husband became too ill to continue in the position. He died in 1928. Although she served ably as superintendent, Mrs. Beam was heard to remark, "I prefer the role of just plain teacher, as I miss the direct contact with the boys and girls I love."

After her two years as superintendent, Mrs. Beam returned to the classroom, where she remained until her retirement in 1945. In all, she would spend fifty-eight years as a teacher.

When Mrs. Beam retired from the Bethel Hill School in 1942, at the age of seventy-five, former students presented "Mama," as she was affectionately called, a silver plaque inscribed as a token of appreciation "for a life of loving service to the Bethel Hill community."

Her retirement was only in the technical sense, though, for she continued to teach, sometimes for months at a time, as a substitute at Bethel Hill and other schools in Person County.

In addition to teaching, Mrs. Bea (as she came to be known) founded the Parent Teacher Association of Person County. She also held several offices in the North Carolina Association of Educators, Person County chapter.

She died in 1951 at the age of eighty-four after suffering a broken hip.

Written by Phyliss Boatwright.

Sources: The Courier-Times *Centennial Edition, 1982, sec. H14;*

Bethel Hill School 1999–2000.

Cuningham with One *N*

Cunningham Township occupies Person County's northwestern-most corner. It has undergone a substantial makeover since its earliest days of recorded history.

The earliest documents come from Colonel William Byrd of Virginia, who led a surveying party in 1728 to determine the dividing line between North Carolina and Virginia. This party made its way through what became the Cunningham Township in October of that year. A summarized account of the journey compiled by Preston Satterfield tells the tale of the first buffalo ever shot in the state, which happened to be in Person County. Byrd, while camped near Cunningham, also made a journal entry about the presence of wolves.

A lot of interesting people have come out of the Cunningham region, according to Person County historian Mrs. Jean Newell. In fact, the township was named after one of its earliest settlers, Alexander Cuningham. Note the name of the family is spelled with one "n," while the accepted spelling of the township as shown on maps has two.

In 1799, Alexander Cuningham built Waverly Hall, and the family home continues to be owned by a descendant of the Cuningham patriarch. At that time, Waverly was called "Hall" while today it is referred to as "Waverly Plantation." Waverly Plantation was listed on the National Register of Historic Places in 1974 and restored in the 1980s. At this same time the family cemetery was cleaned, the brush cleared and tombstones set upright, and a listing of the names from the tombstones was compiled.

An Episcopal Church once stood on the grounds of the plantation. Alexander Cuningham built the building so the family could attend worship services. The structure stood until 1981, when it became too dangerous to occupy and was dismantled.

In addition to the church and home, the plantation also included a general store located near the house and situated close by the railroad tracks.

Though Joseph T. Tingen's name may not be familiar, most Personians would probably recognize his songs. Cunningham township resident Tingen was born in 1839 and enlisted in the Confederate Army in 1862, where he served for a period as a bandmaster under General Robert E. Lee.

It was during this era that Tingen wrote the songs "Sweet Bye and Bye" and "God Be With You," which he dedicated to his mother with the words "To Mer." The story continues that he loaned these songs to another band member, and after the Civil War ended the music was published, but not by Tingen. Credit for the words and music went to a William Tomer.

Tingen's repertoire of songs included music about his home county, including "The Person County Quickstep," which he dedicated to Dr. Terrell in appreciation of what the benefactor had done for the county.

Other families that lived in the Cunningham Township in the late 1800s had names that remain familiar today: Powell, McGehee, Williams, Pointer, Jones, Barker, Stanfield, Faulkner, Newman, Shanks and Dixon.

Several churches have early roots in Cunningham Township, including New Ephesus Church, which was situated on land donated by John Cuningham.

A similarly-named church is Ephesus Primitive Baptist Church, founded in 1834 with the original structure having been located across the road from its present location near McGehee's Mill. Ephesus is the mother church for Semora; Alton, Virginia; and Lamberth Memorial Baptist churches.

Concord United Methodist Church is also located in Cunningham Township near the Olive Hill Township line. Organized in 1815, the congregation built a new wood frame church in 1857. In 1908, this second church building was moved across the road and became a store. This building burned about 1946. The present Concord church was built in 1908 on the original site.

Written by Vicki Berry.

Originally appeared in the Courier-Times, *March 9, 2005, sec. B1.*

The Doctor Who Funded Schools and Delivered a Powerful Message

Apparently Dr. John C. Terrell, born and raised in the Cunningham community of Person County, believed fully in the adage "What goes around comes around."

Born into poverty in a one-room house on September 30, 1818, Terrell grew up with little except for his determination. He somehow knew that education was the only way to better himself and sought help from the wealthy and educated in his community. He was refused that aid, however, and would never forget the slight.

Terrell did find one friend, though, who saw and respected the determination the young man displayed. John W. Cunningham sent Terrell to school in Leasburg to study under Solomon Lea. Terrell went on to the University of Pennsylvania in Philadelphia and received his medical degree on April 3, 1840.

A highway marker denotes the birthplace of Dr. John C. Terrell, a major benefactor to public schools in Person County.

The young Dr. Terrell returned to his home and began practicing in the Cunningham community, using the log house in which he grew up as an office, where he treated both the wealthy and the poor. When he had been back home for three years, his father, Thomas Terrell, died. Dr. Terrell continued living with his mother and brother Tom while building a nice home for his bride-to-be about a mile from his family home. However, his fiancée died before they could wed, and Terrell was so devastated by the loss that he never moved into the house.

He continued his medical practice, though, through the Civil War years. With cash in short supply during the war, Terrell accepted notes from the big plantation owners in the county in return for his services as a physician. When the war was over and it became obvious that the notes would never be repaid, Terrell decided to show those formerly wealthy landowners who refused to help him in his youth that what goes around does indeed come around. He moved back to Philadelphia, where his nieces lived, and began foreclosing on homes and holdings back in Cunningham. After General Lee's surrender, several of Cunningham's former plantation owners suddenly found themselves homeless.

But just as he remembered the wrongs he had suffered, Terrell also never forgot those who helped him. When the aging Colonel Cunningham was dying, Terrell returned to Person County to care for him.

During one of Cunningham's earlier visits to Terrell in Philadelphia, the two visited Gerard College, and Terrell got the idea to endow the schools in his home county. He gave about $50,000 to have schools built in each of the districts throughout Person County and bequeathed the rest of his estate to the public school fund. The Terrell Fund is still aiding local public schoolchildren today.

According to a March 31, 1897 article in the *Courier*, Terrell practiced medicine in Philadelphia until 1868, "and stood high as a physician. He visited Richmond several times during the war to minister to the needs of the sick and wounded in the hospitals."

He was a successful businessman and financier as well as a doctor, the article states. "He leaves an estate valued at between $75,000 and $100,000, and which consists chiefly of first-class securities…His will directs that over $40,000 shall go to the public schools of Person County, and he also desires sufficient funds in addition to be used in building an academy in each of the twenty-six school districts of the county…The donation for the Person County schools, we are informed, is the largest ever made by any individual for a similar purpose in the history of North Carolina."

An editorial, also in the March 31, 1897 *Courier*, states that Terrell's act was "truly noble. The will has not been probated yet, and we don't know what the provisions are, but it is supposed this money was left as an endowment, which, if such is the case, will insure free schools at least eight months in the year for every district in county. In addition to this he made provision for school buildings in each district…

"In years to come, when other names will be forgotten Dr. Terrell will be a household word and only sung to be praised."

Written by Phyliss Boatwright.

Sources: The Courier-Times *Centennial Edition, 1982, sec. D12; Stuart Wright,* Historical Sketch of Person County *(Danville, NC: The Womack Press, 1977).*

Elko Dairy and Foushee Barn

In 1985, Roxboro resident James Hazel was going about the business of clearing a lot near Evelyn Day Road when he came across the top of a bottle sticking out of the ground.

Then he discovered the writing on the glass, "Mrs. E.B. Foushee—Elko Dairy Farm, Roxboro, NC."

In addition to the pint bottle, he also exposed a quart-size milk bottle that included the name "Elko Dairy" along with the words "PROUD PARENTS KNOW THE IMPORTANCE OF SAFE MILK" with the painting of a man and a toddler.

"I was surprised it was in such good shape — not broken and not chipped. That is what surprised me," emphasized Hazel.

"I asked a bunch of friends around here if they could remember the dairy," he said. "People could remember the dairy but didn't remember when it existed."

After keeping the bottles around his house for the past twenty years, Hazel said he became concerned that the bottles would get broken and was prompted to take them to the Person County

Museum of History. At the same time, he hoped to learn a little more about the dairy.

At the museum, the pint- and quart-sized milk bottles joined another Elko Dairy quart bottle that had been donated to the museum the previous year by Elbert Evans.

The trio of bottles spurred Museum Exhibit Committee member Jean Newell to delve into the past and find out as much as she could about the Foushee dairy farm and Elko Dairy for the museum's "Homegrown Business" exhibit. She admits to having a head start, since she and her husband owned the former Foushee barn situated at the end of Burch Street.

"Mrs. E.B. Foushee had a dairy farm and was a supplier of milk for the Elko Dairy in the late 1930s, all of the 1940s and the early 1950s," said Newell.

The distribution point for Elko Dairy was located on North Main Street at the spot used today by Young Monument Company.

"Elko Diary went around and picked up milk in the large metal milk cans," said Newell, "then processed the milk and bottled it."

From this Main Street location, the dairy also sold ice cream, ice cream sodas and malted milk to folks who stopped by the store, as well as bottles of milk to anyone who needed extra.

Newell finds it unusual that Mrs. E.B. Foushee would have had her name placed on glass bottles, and she believes that there might have been other locally owned dairy farms that did the same.

Elko Dairy also ceased operating in the 1950s, when Long Meadow Dairy in Rougemont expanded into surrounding areas, including Roxboro. After Mrs. Foushee ceased supplying milk, around 1954, Henry Newell Sr. bought the barn.

After the Newells bought it, the barn was used as a sweet potato processing plant. Farmers throughout the county brought sweet potatoes to the barn where they were washed, graded, waxed and put in bushel baskets ready for market, explained Mrs. Newell.

From the barn, trucks hauled the sweet potatoes north to New York for four years, until a nematode created a problem for sweet potato farmers. She explained that then-County Extension Agent Wayland Reams worked with farmers to try to rid the soil of the problem, but it was ultimately the nematode that put a halt to the barn's use for sweet potato processing

The structure then housed a pillow manufacturing business as the Newells began producing sofa pillows using "waste" upholstery from Collins & Aikman. Pillow manufacturing continued until the mid-1970s.

For the past thirty years, the barn has been used for storage.

Newell admits, "It was the pint milk bottle that started me down memory lane."

But perhaps the building's most colorful history even preceded its life as a dairy barn. In the early 1900s, the barn housed a whisky dispensing facility, or distillery, operated by Colonel Dan Andrews, one of Roxboro's most colorful figures in his own right, explained Newell.

"Colonel Dan also ran a saloon on Depot Street. Actually he ran several saloons," she added. "And at that time, in order for him to legally sell liquor in Roxboro, it had to be produced within Roxboro."

Andrews was a "real character," said Newell.

"People liked Colonel Dan," and, perhaps it was his charisma that influenced city officials to incorporate the barn into the city so he could legally sell his alcoholic beverage.

From distillery to dairy barn to sweet potato processing plant and sofa pillow manufacturing business, the little bottle dug from the ground is part of a storied history from Roxboro's past.

Written by Vicki Berry.

Originally appeared in the Courier-Times, *March 18, 2006, sec. B1.*

The Ghosts of Cothran's Inn

During the mid-1700s the countryside was dotted with way stations that offered travelers a place to stop and rest for the night. Cothran's Inn, in what is now the Gordonton community of Person County, was one such station—but legend has it that many travelers who checked into Cothran's Inn never checked out.

Horseback riders and stagecoaches traveling from Boston, Virginia, to Hillsborough would stop in Milton and at Cothran's Inn in an isolated spot of what is now southwestern Person County. During the eighteenth century, this was a part of the Orange territory.

The building was impressive, with framing timbers numbered at the corners with Roman numerals. The timbers, which had been cut elsewhere, were assembled, much like a puzzle, to form Cothran's Inn. According to *Person County Folklore: The Rock and the Nail*, in 1994 the numerals could still be seen where the corner joints were formed. As with many other buildings of the time, the kitchen at Cothran's Inn was separate from the main house in case of fire. The first floor of the main building contained a large ordinary—a room where travelers could register, sit by the fire, have a drink and relax after a long day on the road. The second floor offered rooms for sleeping, and a large third-floor room was set aside for "extra travelers" who were oftentimes never seen nor heard from again.

Legend has it that the proprietor of the inn, Mr. Cothran, was a greedy man. Whenever a traveler on horseback came through, Cothran would carefully inspect both man and mount in order to assess the value of horse, saddle and the amount of money the man might be carrying in the bag he wore on his belt. Should Cothran decide the traveler was well-off or the mount valuable enough, the unlucky rider would be housed on the third floor of the inn. During the night, Mr. Cothran would kill the traveler and, with the help of his manservant, place the body in a well. The saddle was then hidden and the horse placed in a pasture deep in the woods. The victim's moneybag, of course, was emptied by Cothran, and the horse and saddle were sold to future travelers who needed fresh mounts.

According to legend, Cothran got his manservant to go along with the scheme by promising him his freedom. But each time the servant asked, he was told, "Not yet." After years of hearing "not yet," the manservant refused to go along with another dastardly deed. He demanded his freedom, and Cothran flew into a rage.

Fearing for his life, the servant fled across the woods to a Mr. Gordon's home and confessed all. Gordon gathered a vigilante group and confronted Cothran. It is not known whether Cothran fled or was hung from the nearest tree. The servant had his freedom and left the area after Gordon bought the inn from him.

Gordon ran the inn for a while, and a store was built nearby. Later, the area would come to be known as Gordonton long before Roxboro, now Person County's only incorporated town, was formed.

Mr. Gordon's son remodeled the inn, painted it white and brought his bride to live in what was reportedly the county's first white house.

At the top of the stairs leading to the third floor, it is said a spot—supposedly a bloodstain from an unlucky traveler—can still be seen. Although the board has been scrubbed and bleached until part of the wood is worn away, the spot still reappears when the wood is dry.

Legend has it one can still see and hear activity around the old inn. But to do so, one must visit the inn on a dark night and sit very still and quietly. If one waits long enough, it is said, a flickering candle will appear in a first-floor window. The candlelight disappears quickly but soon shows up again in the garret room, where it hovers for a spell. The light then moves downstairs, where it disappears again. If one is brave enough to wait longer, the hooves of horses will eventually be heard riding away. After another wait, the sound of hooves returns, this time seemingly traveling back toward the inn. This is said to be the ill-fated traveler's horse being taken to pasture, and the rider of the second horse returning to the inn.

The spirits of the travelers who were killed and thrown into the well supposedly still exist as well. During the 1960s, the dirt road that passed Cothran's Inn was paved. This road runs south from Highway 49 toward Wheeler's Church in the Hurdle Mills area of the county. The widened road reached out to the well that Cothran is supposed to have used to hide the bodies of his slain men.

A few months after the Gordonton road was paved, a hole appeared where the well had been covered by asphalt. The highway maintenance crew reportedly went out and covered the spot again, but in two weeks' time, the hole was back. The crew returned, doing a more thorough job. But soon a saucer-shaped indentation the size of the top of the well appeared. Even today, riding north from Wheeler's Church to Highway 49, drivers can feel a dip in the road as the car crosses the well.

Written by Phyliss Boatwright .

Sources: Person County Folklore: The Rock and the Nail *(Raleigh: North Carolina State University, Humanities Extension/Publications, 1994).*

Oscar Scott Woody: *Titanic* Dedication

Person County mail clerk Oscar Scott Woody, who perished on the White Star Liner R.M.S. *Titanic* on April 14, 1912, showed such dedication to his job that the main post office in Roxboro was recently renamed the Oscar Scott Woody Post Office in his honor. Woody received the posthumous recognition on July 12, 2004, when Thirteenth U.S. District Congressman Brad Miller formally announced the post office name change in front of Woody's descendants. Woody is the only United States Postal Service employee ever to have a post office named in his honor.

Woody was one of five mail clerks, three from the United States and two from England, who sailed on the *Titanic*, which was a mail ship. According to Mrs. Jean Newell, docent at the Person County Museum of History, Woody had to "jump through a lot of hoops" to garner the coveted assignment. He and his fellow mail clerks worked "down in the bottom of the ship," Newell says, while above them travelers reveled at being on the massive ship's maiden voyage.

What makes Woody's story "heart wrenching" to Newell is the fact that April 15 would have been the young mail clerk's forty-fourth birthday. His co-workers were giving him a small party just before midnight on that fateful Sunday when the *Titanic* struck an iceberg and began sinking. The men then "went into a panic," Newell says, to save the bags of mail they were responsible for.

Woody and the other clerks worked diligently, Newell says, to save the mail in their charge. They lugged large bags of letters up on deck from where the mail was stored in the bowels of the ship. The mail was sorted into stacks and wrapped in bands that identified the clerk who handled it. When Woody's body was later recovered, one of the mail bands was found in his pocket, along with his watch and a letter he had written to his wife of just eighteen months.

The *Titanic* was en route to New York from Queenstown when it struck the iceberg near Cape Race, going down with over 1,200 passengers still on board. Out of the total passenger roster of 2,201, only 712 were rescued by the *Carpathia*.

After his body was found, personal items were removed and stored to be delivered to next of kin, and Woody was buried at sea, never to return to his native Person County.

His young wife, Leelia Bullard Woody, who was originally from Fredericksburg, Virginia, was not considered next of kin by the United States government. Congress voted to send Woody's personal belongings to his parents, after being sent to the RMS *Dormitory* for transport to America. Each family of mail clerks who died on the *Titanic* also received $2,000.

Leelia Woody sued the White Star Line for $50,000 for pain and suffering and $100 for the cost of her late husband's belongings. However, she never received any compensation.

Written by Phyliss Boatwright.

Sources: *Mrs. Jean Newell and the* Titanic *exhibit at the Person County Museum of History.*

Person County Training School

As was the case with many things at the time, African Americans in Person County found it difficult to get an education during the early part of the twentieth century. But thanks to an organization called the Progressive League and members Dr. R.A. Bryce, M.C. Cooke, Eugene Jeffers, Dr. J.E. Pittman, Stephen Thomas, C.T. Trotter and P.D. Johnson, the Person County Training School was born, allowing black children the chance to study.

In 1925 the school opened its doors as the first public high school for African Americans in the community. It was a union school, serving children in grades one through eleven. Person County Training School's first building was in the Olive Hill community and contained six rooms on two floors. There was also a cottage that could be used as a teacherage, or dormitory.

In 1928 the Progressive League solicited donations of about $1,100 with which to construct a new building, and at the beginning of the new year in 1930, Person County Training School opened its doors and enrollment grew from forty-five to one hundred thirty-six. That year, the fifth in the school's existence, it won accreditation and was rated in Class II-A. Thus, the class of 1930 became the first African Americans in Person County to graduate from an accredited high school.

Person County Training School operated as an accredited institution until 1950. Courses included health, sociology, economics, French and business. Among other extracurricular opportunities, the school offered a debating club, drama club, student council, National Honor Society chapter and 4-H club.

Mary Lester, a Person County Training School student, became the first black girl from the county to appear on television to demonstrate her 4-H project. Another student, Arnie Bass, was awarded a trip to Japan for his work in 4-H.

In 1941, student Richard Yancey, a senior, gave up the chance to receive a diploma, becoming the first African American in Person County to volunteer in the armed services during World War II.

Alumni of the Person County Training School include Clifton R. Jeffers, class of 1952, who earned a law degree, was appointed deputy attorney general in California and headed the Consumer Fraud Unit in San Francisco. He also served as assistant regional administrator for the Housing and Urban Development agency in California.

Jasper R. Clay, class of 1950, received a graduate degree in psychology and did other graduate work in several areas. He became a commissioner with the Maryland Parole Commission.

Mercer Z. Ray, class of 1933, received a degree in business from North Carolina A&T University and rose to an executive position with Golden State Mutual Insurance in California, after working with North Carolina Mutual Life Insurance Company in Winston-Salem.

James C. Owen, class of 1933, received his undergraduate degree from Shaw University, returned to the training school to teach biology, served in World War II, then earned his doctor of dentistry from Meharie Medical College and returned as the first black dentist in Roxboro. In 1969, Dr. Owens was the first African American elected to city council in Roxboro.

After 1950, Person County High School replaced the training school. Linda Clayton Jones, an honors graduate in the class of 1967, went on to North Carolina Central University, majoring in chemistry with minors in biology and math. She graduated with honors in 1971 and entered Duke University Medical School. As a Duke student, Jones developed an interest in the study of cancer and was selected as one of eleven medical students in the United States to study oncology at the National Institutes of Health in Bethesda, Maryland. Returning to Duke, Dr. Jones continued her residency in obstetrics and gynecology and pursued the subspecialty of gynecologic oncology. She was the first woman and first African American to do so.

Written by Phyliss Boatwright.

Sources: Person County Heritage *(1981): 105–110; telephone interview with Linda Clayton Jones.*

The Roxboro Colts: Baseball Team and More

The Roxboro Colts were organized in 1949 to fill a void.

Roxboro had had a black semi-pro baseball team before: Ambrose Lee held the Roxboro Tigers together for a few seasons prior to 1949. But baseball season was fast approaching, and the Tigers were apparently a thing of the past.

Melvin Bates and the late Alex Robinson stepped in to fill the void. They formed the Roxboro Colts.

"Ambrose had had a team for two or three years before that," Bates recalled, "but he wasn't going to have a team that year. There wasn't a team in Roxboro then."

Thus, the Colts were born. Even Bates admits that the foal attempted to walk too quickly.

"It was pretty bad at first," Bates remembered. "We were looking terrible in our first two or three games, got beat pretty bad. It was all local boys back then. Skink Browning [athletic coach at the old Person County High School] was here then and one afternoon we went to Durham and got four players out of

Durham—Wick Springfield, shortstop; Artis Plummer, second base; Henry Campbell, catch; and Harley Page, third base. We took those out-of-towners and beat just about everybody else we played, after losing those first three games."

Bates beamed when he recalled that the Jacksonville (Florida) Eagles of the old American Negro Association were among those victims. In the meantime, the Roxboro Tigers had been reactivated, and the Colts included them among their victims.

The Colts played in a league only once during their several seasons of existence. The league included, in addition to the Colts, Virginia teams Richmond, Hopewell and Danville and North Carolina team Kinston.

"We were in a league just one year, but mostly we played independent ball," said Bates. "The league folded; it was just scattered too far.

"We played a few Sunday games at the old fairgrounds…but most of our games were played at Rocket Park [then the old Roxboro High School field]. We'd have some great crowds too."

The Colts averaged playing twenty-four to twenty-five games per summer.

During all of their years of competition, the Colts were managed by Bates. During most of those years, the team included five or six Person County players, with other players brought in from outside. Durham and some neighboring Virginia towns contributed heavily to the talent of the Colts.

1954 was a banner year for the Colts. They became the first black team to ever participate in the North Carolina State Semi-Pro Baseball Tournament, which was then and now a fixture in Roxboro.

The Colts went on to play a total of six tournaments. They finished fifth out of sixteen teams in 1954, third in 1955 and lost their first two tournament games in 1956. In 1957 the Colts finished eighth.

The Colts did not enter the tournament in 1958 or 1959, but came back in 1960 to place eighth. After sitting out the 1961 event, the Colts placed fifth in 1962, their final tournament year.

"We did pretty well in the tournament," said Bates. "It seemed like we always lost on Friday night. [The championship round was played the following night.] The first time we were in the tournament, we won right up until we played Camp Lejeune." The Camp Lejeune Marines went on to win the state championship.

"Part of the reason for [the demise of the Colts]" said Bates, "was that Central University, North Carolina College [in Durham], it was called then, dropped baseball and that was where we were getting a number of our players. We stopped getting in the tournament because we didn't have the caliber of players to compete."

But in their heyday, the Colts certainly did.

"The Colts carried a lot of respect in Roxboro and Person County," Bates said. "We didn't have just black people attending the games. We had good attendance, and a lot of our fans were white. From time to time, we had some white ball players, too.

"We played pretty good baseball, and we were well-recognized in Roxboro and Person County."

The North Carolina State Semi-Pro Baseball Tournament began in 1935 and moved to Roxboro in 1950. The tournament was still a fixture in the city when the above article was written in 1982.

The first semi-pro event was staged at the old Rocket Park and was sponsored by the Roxboro Exhibition Company. About twenty years later, the Roxboro Optimist Club became the sponsor, and shortly thereafter the grandstand at the park was demolished. The club built its own park, dubbing it Optimist Park.

Written by Winkie Wilkins.

Originally appeared in the Courier-Times *Centennial Edition, 1982, sec. H7.*

The Kirbys and Person County Entertainment

In 1973 the Kirby Theatre on Roxboro's Main Street closed, leaving the city and county for nearly thirty years with no choice but to drive thirty miles to Durham or Danville, Virginia, to see a show.

On December 20, 1973, the *Courier-Times* ran the following article by staff writer Winkie Wilkins:

> *Forty-five years of motion picture history for the Kirby family will come to an end here on Monday, December 31, when the Kirby Theatre will present its final movie.*
>
> *The entire theater building has been purchased by Person County and will be used in the future as a civic center and office building.*
>
> *The final movie to be screened at the Kirby will be* That Darn Cat*, a Walt Disney production.*
>
> *"We have always tried to present good family entertainment," said Mrs. Nita Kirby Morgan, the theater's manager, "and we felt that a Disney production would be a good one to close with."*

The Kirby Theatre in 1982. Today the building on Roxboro's Main Street houses the Kirby Civic Auditorium and the Person County Arts Council.

Mrs. Morgan, daughter of the late Teague Kirby, has managed the theater since her father's death in 1970. Prior to that time, she was her father's "right-hand man."

Teague Kirby was one of the originators of the Kirby Brothers Company, which began in the theater business in 1918. He founded the company along with his brother Cy and two other brothers. In later years, two brothers dropped out of the organization, leaving Teague and Cy as the owners.

The Kirby Brothers initially entered the theater business by purchasing the Princess Theater from Matt Long. That theater was located at the present site of Thompson-Allen Insurance Agency [on Main Street].

In 1924 the Kirbys built the Palace Theater and closed the Princess Theater. The Palace, which remained in operation until March 3, 1957, was located at the present location of Green's Jewelers [also on Main Street].

During those same years, the Kirbys owned theaters in Oxford, Wake Forest, and South Hill, Virginia. However, all three theaters were closed during the Great Depression of the 1930s.

The former Palace Theater on Roxboro's Main Street is the namesake for today's Palace Pointe entertainment complex on U.S. 501 South.

In 1936 the Kirby Brothers built a second theater, the Dolley Madison, located in the present location of Person Furniture Company [on the opposite side of Main Street]. From that time until the closing of the Palace in 1957, the Kirbys operated both theaters.

The opening of the present Kirby Theatre had been planned for several years before it became a reality. Construction of the Kirby building, including the theater, Main Street business establishments and second-floor offices had been started in the early 1940s. The Main Street Shops were completed and ready for occupancy in 1941. However, World War II prevented the completion of the theater and the second floor. The war took so many people out of Person County that the Kirbys feared they would not be able to make their investment in the theater pay. Thus, construction was delayed until the post-war years.

Finally, the Kirby Theatre was completed in 1949. The Dolley Madison was closed on Saturday, July 30, the Kirby opened on Monday, August 1, and for the next nine years both the Kirby and the Palace were in operation. The first motion picture shown was The Stratton Story, starring James Stewart and June Allyson.

The movie, which featured the life of Monty Stratton, a major league baseball pitcher who lost a leg in a hunting accident and attempted a comeback on an artificial limb, drew large crowds and attracted attention from some of the persons involved.

On the eve of the opening, the Kirbys received a telegram from June Allyson. The telegram read, "Jimmy [Stewart] and I are so delighted that you will open your new Kirby Theatre with The Stratton Story."

Another telegram came from Stratton and stated, "As a southern boy, I am very pleased that a southern theater will open its doors for the first time with The Stratton Story. Thank you very much."

During the remainder of the summer of 1949, the Kirby Theatre presented nine other motion pictures. Among them were Mr. Belvedere Goes to Washington, starring Clifton Webb, and Ma and Pa Kettle, starring Percy Kilbride and Marjorie Main.

But of all the movies ever to show at the Kirby during its twenty-four-year history, Gone with the Wind has been the biggest attraction. In the various Kirby theaters, the movie has played thirteen times since its premiere in 1940. It last played here in May of 1972. Jesse James, starring Henry Fonda and Tyrone Power, has shown a dozen times and The Return of Frank James, with the same two leading actors, has played nine times.

The longest run ever made by a single movie at the Kirby was by The Sound of Music, which played for three weeks in 1967.

Personal appearances by stars at the Kirby also played a big role in the theater's past. Some of those to make appearances were Al "Fuzzy" St. John, Lash LaRue, Little Jimmy Dickens, Lester Flat and Earl Scruggs, Tim McCoy, Tom Mix and Whip Wilson.

> *All drew large crowds, but according to Mrs. Morgan, St. John set the all-time single performance attendance record at the Kirby.*
>
> *However, it will all come to an end on December 31, 1973. After four theaters, thousands of movies, mountains of hot popcorn, a million tears and a billion laughs, the Kirby family will entertain Personians no more.*

In 2000 a group of investors built an entertainment complex on U.S. Highway 501, just south of Roxboro. The complex is called Palace Pointe, and its main attraction is the Palace Theatre, so-named for the old Palace uptown.

The Kirby was restored in 1999 and today offers patrons Broadway-style shows, musicals and children's productions. Every other year, the Kirby hosts the Red Stocking Revue, a fundraiser for the Roxboro Women's Club. The theater building also houses the county Arts Council and gallery.

Written by Winkie Wilkins.

Originally appeared in the Courier-Times *Centennial Edition, 1982, sec. G15.*

A Place Called Wolf

Although Roxboro is the only incorporated town, there are many communities scattered throughout the twenty-mile-by-twenty-mile square of land known as Person County.

One of the lesser known is the community once located three-and-a-half miles northeast of Roxboro known as Wolf. Today what was once a tiny village is nothing more than a small garden area called Wolf's Corner. Nevertheless, many unexplained events over the years make the former community of Wolf an interesting part of Person County history.

Christine Slaughter Rogers, the wife of former Person County Schools Superintendent Dr. David Rogers, was born and raised in Wolf and wrote the book, *Tales of Wolf in Person County, North Carolina*, in 2002.

According to Rogers's book, Nuptial Blair Slaughter founded the Wolf community shortly after the Civil War ended. The seventeen-year-old's father, Jacob, gave him two hundred acres of land and a horse and told him to get out on his own. Woods were cleared and a house was built close to a winding dirt road that bordered the Roxboro and Allensville townships. There, N.B. "Tonch" Slaughter raised a family and tobacco. He built a store and founded a one-room school inside the store so that his children could receive an education. Later N.B. Slaughter's store also housed a post office. The post office began, according to Rogers's family history, when Slaughter and others in Wolf experienced difficulty getting their mail. Slaughter applied to Washington, D.C., and was granted permission to operate a post office. He rode horseback to Roxboro to pick up the mail and bring it back to the community. The post office was dubbed Wolf, according to Slaughter family lore, because there was a wolf den in the field between the N.B. Slaughter home and the store where he located the post office. Today, a descendant of N.B. Slaughter lives in the original residence and a wall dividing two rooms retains evidence of the slots into which mail was separated.

Slaughter also founded a church—Rock Grove Baptist—and ran a blacksmith shop.

N.B. Slaughter's first wife, Martha Anne Hicks, gave him thirteen children before her death in 1897 at age forty-seven. A year after Martha Anne died, Tonch married his cousin, Lucy E. Slaughter of Granville County.

In July 1898, Rufus Slaughter, the oldest son of Tonch and Martha Anne, became very ill and was taken to the hospital in Raleigh since there was no hospital in Roxboro. He wanted badly to come home, according to Rogers's history. As he grew sicker, the family back home began hearing unexplained noises that sounded like hammers and chains beating against the tin roof. In fact, the noises were so loud and continuous that they drew attention from neighbors.

The noises finally ended after Rufus's brother Vanus took his gun outside and shot over the housetop several times. Rufus died a few days later, at the age of twenty-eight, and was buried in the

Rock Grove Cemetery at midnight, due to the fear of spreading the typhoid fever that killed him.

Many tragedies and strange occurrences happened in Wolf over the years. Sometime around 1905, a man who worked as a tenant farmer for Tonch was heard screaming in the Slaughter home. When Tonch's sons Chummie and Offie ran from the field to check on the situation, they found the man in a chimney corner on the side of the house. The man had probably suffered a seizure and fell helpless into the open fire. Tonch's daughter Rachel would later relate that her brothers stopped her from going close to the house to protect her from seeing a man "whose eyes have literally burned out of his head."

In 1930 a thirteen-year-old girl, Bessie Mae Yarboro, was killed instantly in front of the Wolf store after getting off the school bus. The driver of an approaching county-owned truck failed to stop, hitting the child while her mother watched from a bedroom window in her home.

Moses T. "Chummie" Slaughter, who lived in the family home and ran the store after his father died, was murdered there on Christmas Eve, 1964. At the age of eighty-five, Chummie was beaten during the robbery of the store. He died a week later, due to complications from three skull fractures and a subsequent stroke. A week before he died, however, Chummie's seven-year-old grandson dreamed he was playing cards with his grandfather and Chummie told him, "I must go; my time is up."

Rachel Slaughter never married and died in her childhood home, in the same room where she was born, at the age of ninety-eight. Christine Rogers writes that on a cold winter night in 1979 she received a phone call from the woman who spent nights at the Slaughter home after Rachel grew old.

Mrs. Breedie Hughes told Rogers, "If I was a scary person I wouldn't stay with Miss Rachel" because "the place is haunted." Hughes then told Rogers that a few weeks before Miss Rachel's death, the two women were watching TV when they heard a knock on the front door. The house had four outside doors, and no one had used the front door for years. When Hughes checked to see who was knocking, there was no one at the door. The knocks continued, however, and Hughes saw a blue shadow pass across the door. When the knock came again, Hughes tried to open the door but felt a force against it. When she told Miss Rachel that she thought the house was haunted, the calm reply was that "when these things happen, it simply means a family member is going to die."

About two weeks later, sitting by the window in her bedroom, Rachel died suddenly from a stroke.

Generations of Slaughters have lived in the area once known as Wolf. Christine Rogers now lives near the apple orchard that was first planted during Chummie Slaughter's lifetime. Members of the fifth generation of the N.B. Slaughter family now occupy the original home.

Written by Phyliss Boatwright.
Sources: The Courier-Times, *August 25, 2004, sec. B1; Christine Slaughter Rogers,* Tales of Wolf in Person County, North Carolina.

2–0 Basketball Game Put Person County on National and International Maps

The 1977 basketball game recounted below brought national attention to Person Senior High School and Hillside High in Durham. According to an editor's note in the *Courier-Times* Centennial Edition of 1982, "Virtually every major newspaper in the country carried an account of the game. An account also appeared in a newspaper in Madrid, Spain."

The following article appeared in the *Courier-Times* on February 3, 1977, and was reprinted in the Centennial Edition:

> *Person Senior High and Hillside High of Durham made the national news after their basketball game Tuesday night, but Person coach Reid Davis doesn't know how he should react to the Rockets' 2–0 loss.*
>
> *It was written correctly, and you're reading it correctly. The final score was Hillside 2, Person 0.*

"I just don't know how to feel about it," Davis said. "I don't know how I should feel about it."

The outcome, believe it or not, was decided in the first two seconds of play. Hillside's Leon McCrae took control of the game-opening tip-off and hit on a twenty-foot bank shot with 7:58 remaining on the clock.

The game then stayed scoreless through its remaining 31 minutes and 58 seconds.

"We certainly never intended for it to be a 2–0 ballgame," Davis said. "We intended to spread it out and get Myles (six-foot, six-inch center Anthony) and McRae (a six-foot, five-inch forward) away from the basket."

But, with the 2-0 lead in his pocket, Hillside coach Willie Bradshaw ordered his troops to stay in their zone defense. The one time they came out was in the second quarter. Immediately, the Rockets spread things out and got a lay-up, but Kip Paylor's shot rolled around the rim and dropped off.

The Rockets managed to get the final shot in each of the four periods but just couldn't connect. In the final twenty-eight seconds of play, the Rockets got off three shots, one a lay-up by Ricky Paylor. The final effort of the night was Kip Paylor's corner jumper, which hit the front of the rim and bounded away. It came with one second on the clock.

That sealed the final score at 2–0 and put the Rockets and Hornets in the state record books. No source has been able to turn up a lower score in a basketball game in North Carolina.

The low score is not a national record, however. That record was set in the Illinois state high school tournament in 1930 when Georgetown defeated Homer by a 1–0 score.

While Davis never intended for the Tuesday night contest to turn into an out-and-out stall, he also never imagined that it would. "I was very much surprised that Hillside stayed in the zone," he said.

"I thought they would come out right away...The same thing's been done to us in the past, when we had bigger, stronger teams."

Davis has some concerns about what effect the low-scoring game might have. One of his primary concerns is for his players.

"The thing that bothers me is that some of our players' classmates are probably going to say funny things about being shut out and maybe about not having courage enough to play. Gosh, our kids have played with courage all year.

"The decision was mine and mine alone," Davis continued. "I have to take all responsibility for the decision and the loss. I'm proud of the way our kids carried it out. I think they showed their courage in that they stuck with it so well..."

Davis continued, "I know [the fans] came to see us play basketball, but I think it's my job to provide our kids with their best possible way to win. We've been spreading people out all year, but this is the first time anyone refused to come out."

The Rockets took a total of seven shots for the night and, of course, hit none. Hillside made one of five. There were only six rebounds in the contest, with Hillside capturing five of them.

Article originally appeared in the Courier-Times *Centennial Edition, 1982, sec. H13.*

Northern Person: Hager's Mountain, Bethel Hill and Woodsdale

Hager's Mountain is a natural landmark within the township of Woodsdale that has not changed over the centuries. During the early days of the twentieth century, the site served as a backdrop for Sunday picnic lunch gatherings. The Person County Museum of History indicates that the spelling variations include Hager, Heffie, Hagie, Hage and Hager's. Additionally, early deeds refer to the locale as Aspin Mountain.

Depending on which county map one scrutinizes, the dot denoting the hub of Bethel Hill may be found in Woodsdale Township or in its eastern neighbor, Holloway Township. However, Bethel Hill Charter School, which began around 1888 as Bethel Hill Institute, is situated in Woodsdale Township. Since the school, in its various incarnations over time, is and has been considered the heart of the community, Bethel Hill is most often aligned with Woodsdale.

The 1870 Person County census lists numerous households in the Woodsdale Township involved in farming. Additional occupations listed were tobacco roller, physicians, teachers, retail merchants, blacksmiths, teamster, tobacco steamer, shoemaker, grist miller, house carpenters, tanner and surveyor.

One word is oft-repeated when Bethel Hill is mentioned: education. That's primarily due to the fact that from its earliest days to the present, education and the Bethel Hill School have been the nucleus of the community.

"Bethel Hill is steeped in education," said John Hall, Bethel Hill native and Person County Museum of History board member.

The roots of education in the Bethel Hill community predate the Civil War. The custom of the early 1800s was that education was received in the home or at private or boarding schools because free or public schools did not exist at that time.

Around 1888, Reverend J.A. Beam began construction on the Bethel Hill Institute. A clipping notes that "This was a well-known school that attracted students from many sections of the state as well as South Carolina and Virginia. For seventeen years, until it burned in January 1905, more than 100 ministers were educated there."

Over the ensuing years, the school at Bethel Hill was rebuilt in stages.

Documentation at the Person County Museum of History provides an extensive history of the school, not only in the form of newspaper clippings from over the past century but also publications such as the recent "memory book" entitled *Bethel Hill School 1999–2000*. Additional revealing documents include an early school newspaper called *The Pine Needle* from 1960 and a Future Farmers of America Official Scrapbook covering the year from April 1, 1939, to July 1, 1940.

A program from the 1932 high school graduating class play, *Jumbo Jum*, points out that student thespian Enos Slaughter may have had a career in acting had his baseball career not panned out.

A man stands beside the massive "Loch Lilly Oak" at Chub Lake.

Also included in the school display are photographs of early sports teams including the 1925 football team, which was one of the first in the county. The team wore homemade uniforms while their rival, the Roxboro High team, wore "proper," or store-bought uniforms.

Since the Reverend Beam was instrumental in combining the fields of ministry and education, the Bethel Hill Institute can claim to have trained ministers as well as educated its children. Religion has always played and continues to play a large role in the Bethel Hill community.

According to Stuart Wright's book, *Historical Sketch of Person County*, "In 1727 there was only one Baptist church in the entire state, but by 1790 that number increased to ninety-four churches. The Reverend Harry R. Mathis dates Bethel Hill Baptist church from 1779 but Mrs. J.H. Merritt, in her account of the church history, states that the church 'was constructed with 100 members in 1774. The first structure was destroyed by fire in 1803. In 1832 it underwent extensive repairs and lasted until 1868, when the third church house was erected.'"

According to a history of Shiloh Church, another important church in Bethel Hill, the earliest known mention of Shiloh is in a biographical sketch of Elder Durham Hall. This sketch was included in the minutes of the County Line Baptist Association held at Tar River Church in Granville County in 1861. It recorded that Elder Durham Hall "preached an able and interesting sermon at Shilo, Person County on the twentieth of January 1861...which was the last sermon he ever preached."

The combined general store and post office was often the "unofficial gathering location" for rural communities, not only to socialize with neighbors while picking up the essentials but also to "gather the latest news and gossip," the museum notes.

Bethel Hill had a post office from 1860 to 1914, when it was discontinued to Denniston, Virginia, according to *Person County Heritage*, published by the Person County Historical Society. The postmasters included John Montague, James Woody, Thomas Woody, Ola Woody, John Barrett and Thomas Woody.

According to John Hall, three things stand out in the history of Bethel Hill—education, agriculture and prominent citizens whose roots are traced back to the community.

In addition to the Beam family, notable family names from the Bethel Hill and Woodsdale communities include Brooks, Jones, Humphries, Montague, Jacobs, Crutchfield, Woody, Rogers, Boswell, Fontaine and Day.

Aubrey L. Brooks established a scholarship that continues to benefit Person County college students.

The progress of many rural towns in the late 1800s can often be directly linked to the arrival of the railroad. During that era, the village of Woodsdale could boast a train station. According to documentation compiled by the M.J. Camp Railroad Station Historical Society Inc., the Woodsdale station was situated on the Lynchburg and Durham Railroad line. Built of wood, the station was constructed in 1890.

That station has since been removed, restored and relocated. It now serves as an office adjacent to the Clarksville Station restaurant in Roxboro.

In fact, several of the historic buildings originally within Woodsdale, which was named after the Wood family, have been restored and relocated to Roxboro. The Brooks store and post office, once the core of Woodsdale, is now a component of the Person County Museum of History campus. For many years, J. Bryan Boswell was postmaster and ran the store for the Brookses.

A post office was originally established in Woodsdale in 1833 and served the community until 1975 when it was discontinued to Roxboro. Among the postmasters who served Woodsdale, in addition to Boswell, as listed in *Person County Heritage*, were Hugh Woods, John Rogers, John Rogers Jr., Rachel Mitchell, Edwin J. Robertson, John S. Robert, Buckley Walker, Edwin J. Robertson Jr., Luther C. Pixley, Bernard E. Mitchell, Reuben P. Brooks and Alma H. Brooks.

Another two-story general store in Woodsdale was operated by the Mitchells, who also operated the grist mill. And yet another retail operation in thriving Woodsdale was conducted by R.G. Robertson.

Also reported to have been located in the center of Woodsdale was the Woodsdale Community School, a Masonic Lodge building that was also used as a school for black children from 1927 to 1955.

Woodsdale resident, ninety-five-year-old Luna J. Drumwright, recalls substitute teaching at the school, which still stands alongside Woodsdale Road.

Mollie Beam taught at the Bethel Hill Institute before making history as the first female superintendent of schools.

"It was a three-room," she recalled. And she remembers filling in for the second, third and seventh grades. "There was no running water and no electricity, but we learned so much," said Ruth Royster, who attended the Woodsdale Community School in the early 1940s.

In the 1940s, Drumwright also worked as a secretary for the Woodsdale Funeral Home, owned by the Brooks family.

A more recent establishment in the community was the Woodsdale Animal Hospital, which has since relocated to Roxboro but has retained the name, thus indicating its roots.

Woodsdale was quite a social hub in its day. Part of that social scene included Saturday afternoon ballgames, according to Woodsdale native Royster. The games were played on the school lot beginning in the spring of each year.

"Ballgames were a big thing up until the 1960s," she recalls, explaining that spectators could buy soda, snowballs and homemade ice cream while watching the sport.

While the quiet community of today is less of a social hub than in its heyday, it does claim to be home to one lone business, a sawmilling operation.

Also remaining in the neighborhood of Woodsdale are two African Methodist Episcopal churches.

In 1872 the first Allen Chapel African Methodist Episcopal Church building was built in the Woodsdale community. According to the history of that church, among the parishioners responsible were those with the family names of Bailey, Mitchell, Collett, Clay, Jones and Woods.

Additionally, Bailey's Chapel African Methodist Episcopal Church was built on land that was purchased in 1902 from the Board of Education of the Woodsdale School District. According to church members, the original church building was donated by the Methodists and moved piece by piece to the current location. At one time, there were actually two Bailey's Chapel churches.

Another name from the Woodsdale Township associated with the social scene of yesteryear is Loch Lily, now known to Personians as Chub Lake. The lake existed as early as 1761 as a millpond, and for several years was known as Bull's Mill Pond, later being referred to as Barnett's Pond, after the owners.

In its early days as a major tourist attraction, the lake reportedly drew "hundreds of people for picnics, swimming, camping and fishing."

A post office served the community of Chub Lake for two decades, from 1884 to 1905, when it was discontinued to Woodsdale. Henry G. Clayton and Wiley J. Winstead served as postmasters.

Written by Vicki Berry.

Originally appeared in the Courier-Times, *April 28, 2004, sec. B1.*

The Community of Push

A little knoll in Person County, which required an extra "push" to ascend the incline or get wheels rolling when caught in the sticky mud, may be what gave the rural community of Push its distinctive name. At least, that is the tale current residents of the area say they have heard over the years about the naming of their Flat River Township farming community.

The community with the unusual name was located on the old road that ran between Roxboro and Hillsborough and was known as the Old Hillsborough Road. It ran parallel with the Old Durham Road, "in sight of each other," according to Nat Williams, who currently lives in what was once known as Push. Remnants of the Old Hillsborough Road can still be seen as a depression in a pasture, Williams said.

Though hardly what one would call a thriving metropolis around the turn of the twentieth century, Push did boast a post office, a general store and a blacksmith shop of sorts.

More precisely, the store and post office in Push were located about two hundred yards from the corner of Cates Mill Road and Hurdle Mills Road, though the Hurdle Mills Road had not been established at the time Push existed.

The few modern-day maps that chart the community pinpoint the town on Route 157, the Hurdle Mills Road, south of Payne's Tavern and Allen's Level, in the Flat River Township. According to a May 1900 edition of the Roxboro *Courier*, "Push, between Hurdle Mills and Bushy Fork," had a recently established post office. The mail center was short-lived, however, as the Push post office was discontinued in 1908.

As was often the case before modern-day transportation, rural roadways had few miles separating one country general store from another. The general store served as a community hub where local folks purchased necessities and commodities that were not grown in the garden or produced on the farm. Push was no different and had its own general store, owned by resident George Jones, according to descendant Howard Jones, who currently lives nearby. The Push general store was located on Cates Mill Road, near a crossroads, along with a few other buildings, based on stories Howard Jones recalls hearing as a child.

A ledger from the Push general store, provided by Jones, lists items such as sugar bought for fifty cents, coffee, a pair of shoes that sold for $1.25 and farming hardware that included plow joints. In fact, the Push general store could be considered the forerunner of today's Super Wal-Mart and Target stores. It was a handy marketplace for residents and sold most any item they might need.

In addition to owning the Push general store, George Jones was a member and church secretary of Mount Zion Methodist Church, one of the earliest churches in the southern part of Person County.

The origins of what is today Mount Zion United Methodist Church date back to before 1786. Originally known as Hargis Meeting House, the minutes of the Flat River Primitive Baptist Church, the earliest written records of the church, state that the membership met at Hargis Meeting House in 1786.

The Push post office had as postmaster Nathaniel Williams, who also worked in the general store. In addition to his jobs as store manager and postmaster, Williams also farmed and made repairs to buggies and wagons and, according to descendant Nat Williams, was perhaps also considered the town blacksmith.

Written by Vicki Berry.
Originally appeared in the Courier-Times,
January 12, 2005.

Van Hook Subscription School

The building known as the Van Hook Subscription School is the oldest schoolhouse still standing in Person County and possibly in all of North Carolina. It was built as a school for boys nearly 188 years ago near Paines Tavern by Kindle Van Hook. Van Hook was one of the school's original subscribers, and his name can be found in the agreement between the teacher William Whitefield and the parents of the students. After two moves the school was last located on the Devereaux Davis farm through the family of C.B. Davis.

Students' parents cut the wood for the "central heating system," which was a five-foot square fireplace. The spring down a nearby hill served as the water fountain. The floor was dirt and the windows were holes cut into the walls with no covering to keep out the elements. Desks were directly under the windows and surrounded the room. Holes can be seen in the logs where the desks were connected. Some of the logs have rotted away, making

The Sol O'Briant School replaced the earlier subscription schools after Dr. John C. Terrell died, leaving a sizeable endowment to build and support Person County Schools.

the cabin only seven feet high today. It is difficult to imagine twenty students housed in this one room, which measures only ten-by-fifteen feet.

The teacher agreed to teach five days each week except Election Day and holidays from April 10 to December 25. The subjects taught at first were spelling, reading, writing and arithmetic, and parents were charged five dollars per session per student. Later, classes in gauging, surveying, English, geography and grammar were added but were more expensive to take.

According to Mrs. Jean Newell, docent and exhibits coordinator at the Person County Museum of History, where the Van Hook school building is now located, parents "got smart" about paying the tuition for the school. They would send one child for the first six weeks, that child would teach the second what he had learned, then the second child would go for six weeks, returning to teach his siblings, and so on, until all children in the family had received an education—from the same dollars per session.

When the school was started in 1810, the teacher was only twelve years old. He had learned what he knew from his parents, James and Susanna Minchew Whitefield, and from his own reading. He later became a farmer, justice of the peace and a surveyor. He taught in the Van Hook School until his death in 1857.

The last year of use is uncertain, but records show it was in service up to the Civil War and maybe much longer. One of the last teachers was Miss Harriet Van Hook, a descendant of the school's builder.

Written by Phyliss Boatwright.

Sources: Mrs. Jean Newell; the Person County Museum of History.